THE GREEK TRA

IN NEW TRANSL

GENERAL EDITORS
William Arrowsmith and Herbert Golder

EURIPIDES: Hecuba

EURIPIDES

Hecuba

Translated by
JANET LEMBKE
and
KENNETH J. RECKFORD

New York Oxford
OXFORD UNIVERSITY PRESS
1991

Oxford University Press

Oxford   New York   Toronto
Delhi   Bombay   Calcutta   Madras   Karachi
Petaling Jaya   Singapore   Hong Kong   Tokyo
Nairobi   Dar es Salaam   Cape Town
Melbourne   Auckland

and associated companies in
Berlin   Ibadan

Published by Oxford University Press, Inc.,
200 Madison Avenue, New York, New York 10016

Oxford is a registered trademark of Oxford University Press

Library of Congress Cataloging-in-Publication Data
Euripides.
[Hecuba. English]
Hecuba / Euripides ; translated by Janet Lembke and Kenneth J. Reckford
p. cm. — (The Greek tragedy in new translations)
ISBN 0-19-504251-4 (cloth). — ISBN 0-19-506874-2 (paperback)
1. Hecuba (Legendary character)—Drama. 2. Trojan War—Drama.
I. Lembke, Janet. II. Reckford, Kenneth J., 1933– .
III. Title. IV. Series.
PA3975.H3R43 1991
882′.01—dc20   90-46737
                                                              CIP

9 8 7 6 5 4 3 2
Printed in the United States of America

EDITORS' FOREWORD

If the following line from a lost play—"There is no greater god than necessity"—were all that survived of Euripides, we would have his signature. Poets and philosophers before and after him have said as much: "Even gods do not fight necessity" wrote Simonides; Plato, speaking of Eros, observed: "The necessity of human limbs exceeds that of geometry." But no artist or thinker has ever dramatized with such relentless concentration the pervasiveness of necessity's power, the terrible force by which it destroys character and shapes us to itself. Among those plays preoccupied with this ubiquitous theme, *Hecuba* deserves pride of place.

"Necessity" in English lacks the resonance that *anankē* has in Greek. Its force is still felt in its cognates: *Ang*st, *ang*ina, *anx*iety, *ang*iportus, even *hang*nail. The Greeks often visualized *anankē* as a yoke, a sheer cliff, or a net, but ontologically it implied a vise around the heart, an angina of *being*. The chorus gives us a striking image of this inescapable power at the center of the play, the linchpin between its two actions (for *Hecuba* is one of those plays of shattered theodicy, like *Heracles* and *Andromache*): the first, almost Sophoclean, culminating in the unjustifiable sacrifice of the noble Polyxena; the second involving the brutalization of Hecuba, more atrocity than tragedy. Directly between the two, the chorus dances, so the language strongly suggests, the lockstep of necessity: "My fate gave me to disaster, / my fate gave me over to sorrow / . . . / My grief and a force far stronger— / constraint—come circling around me" (ll. 667–68, 675–76). In the Greek the ode literally begins "for me disaster *had to be* / for me there *had to be* sorrow," in a syncopated rhythm giving prosodic emphasis to the word *khrēn*, "had to *be."* This accent and the corresponding image of encircling, constricting necessity in the antistrophe gave the impression of danced *ananke,* the chorus circling with arms intertwined, closing in on its leader, who presumably mimes an attempt to break free of the chain. Physical slavery has been imposed on the chorus, a necessity as inexorable as old age or death, Dionysus or Aphrodite, powerfully tangible forces (often theatrically present, even personified) that the dramatis personae of Euripides suffer and against which they often struggle.

We *see* the chorus under the yoke of slavery. But by what necessity do the Greek leaders justify the death of Hecuba's daughter, Polyxena, sacrificed to sate Achilles' ghost? Custom requires cattle, not human sacrifice. To justify Polyxena's death in terms of political abstractions, as Odysseus does, is nothing less than monstrous. The chorus's Greek masters have voluntarily enslaved themselves to the mob they purport to lead. They justify their acts in the name of political necessity and by so doing destroy justice and freedom alike. Their complex, sophistic rationalizations are obscene when compared to the simple, barbarian greed of Polymesor, who murders Hecuba's young son for gold. However, against this enslavement to necessity (forced upon Hecuba and the chorus but freely chosen by the Greeks) stands the passion for freedom embodied by Polyxena. Even the Greek army (perhaps not yet as corrupt as their generals cynically believe) has the capacity to be moved by her example. "Set me free so . . . I die free," she says to her captors (l. 583), at which the army roars its approval. She then tears her robe open to the waist, offering herself to the sword, showing "breasts that gleamed like a statue's / carved to honor the gods" (ll. 593–94). In this image of Polyxena, rising divinely above atrocious circumstances, the species's yearning to be free is manifest. Like such other Euripidean youthful heroes and heroines as Alcestis, Iphigeneia, and Makaria, Polyxena reveals the divine in the species.

Her revelation makes the following seem like a Euripidean turn on beauty and the beast. Whereas Hecuba could consent to Polyxena's death and even find a kind of comfort in its nobility, with the discovery of the body of her dead son, Polydorus, washed ashore, the net of *ananke* is irrevocably tightened. Her appeals to justice and compassion are denied by Agamemnon, her suffering brutalizes her, and her atrocious revenge on Polymestor—his two sons dead for one—is correspondingly barbarous. Kneeling as a suppliant before Agamemmnon, Hecuba puts things into perspective: "Like a painter, stand back, / look at me and see my sorrows whole" (ll. 850–51). Formal supplication requires that one person kneel before another with hands outstretched, one reaching toward the chin, the other touching the knee—an image of vulnerability that says "I am wholly in your power," forcing the person in control to recognize in the supplicant the helplessness of the mortal condition that, *mutatis mutandis,* they share. To the Greeks suppliancy was sacrosanct. No gesture more profoundly elicited the compassion arising from that sense of common suffering at the heart of Greek morality. But the "picture" is as troubling as the image of Polyxena facing death was stirring, and Hecuba's plea for pity now becomes a procuress's request for payment. As she reminds Agamemnon of his nights in Cassandra's bed, Hecuba now shockingly begs not for freedom but for revenge. From a "picture of pity," Hecuba becomes Peitho incarnate: "If only Daedalus could work his wonders, / or some god, to give my arms a voice, / my hands a voice, and my hair and feet, / then all would clasp your knees in concert / crying out my plea in all possible ways" (ll. 883–87). Between her painterly image of the suppliant and that of the Daedalean statue, Hecuba names that power "who alone is mankind's queen" (l. 860), Persuasion, whose supreme embodiment is that daimonic Helen hovering over this play like a lethal epiphany: "her eyes flashed, her lovely lustful eyes, and she shamed, / she burnt Troy's blessedness" (ll. 472–73), Hecuba cries at one point; "most beautiful woman on whom / the gold-shining Sun casts light" (l. 674), the chorus (who will curse her in the final ode) intone at another. With Helen we have the supreme image of beauty, *kallos*—the operative moral term in this play—emptied utterly of moral meaning. This is the shape of desire that all men serve: terrible beauty *as* enslaving necessity.

But the real, visible slavery of Hecuba and the chorus starkly reveals and indicts the voluntary slavery of their Greek masters. The real atrocity of *Hecuba* is that none of this *had to* happen. It is the absence of true *anankē* in this play so overwhelmingly concerned with *anankē* that is so disturbing. The bad faith of the Greek leaders destroys any hope, justice, or freedom: "I see that no one alive, no one, is free," says Hecuba. "For some are slaves to money, others to chance / or majority rule or man-made laws / that keep them from acting on their own good sense" (ll. 915–18). Brutal revenge is finally Hecuba's sole passion; she craves it more than freedom, for which she would "be a slave for all the days to come" (l. 797). Not only does character prove corruptible (contrary to Hecuba's own inspired words earlier in the play), but the effect of denying human feeling is her bestial transformation. The reader must visualize the hideousness of the final spectacle: Hecuba gloating over the butchered bodies of the two boys; the blinded Polymestor on all fours, groping to kill her, then prophesying through bleeding eyes of the brutalization to come, as Hecuba is transformed from the *mater dolorosa* of epic into the bitch of Cynossema, the fiery-eyed, hateful fiend of her future.

By anachronizing the myth, projecting the metamorphosis of Hecuba into the play's "present," Euripides gives us a vision of man beneath *anankē*'s yoke as little more—and possibly less—than the automata Hecuba herself describes. Greed and bad faith are behind these abominations. "The harsh necessities of war," Thucydides wrote, "bring most men's characters to a level with their fortunes." This may explain the corruption of Hecuba but not that of her captors, who wear their yoke of slavery freely. By the end of the play, the great moment in which Polyxena seemed to embody the species's passion for freedom appears impossibly far away. The crescendo of brutality into which we are drawn is almost satisfying in its necessitous atrocity. "A man can rise to any heights," T. E. Lawrence once wrote, "but there is a certain animal level beneath which he cannot sink. There is a certainty in degradation, a final safety." This play plummets us to this degrading certainty.

Hecuba requires of its translators scrupulous attention to tonal texture, ranging from grief-stricken monodies and duets to splendidly lyrical choral verse. In addition, there are the problems created by political and forensic rhetoric, by turns colloquially terse and (in the case of the sinister Odysseus and Agamemnon) demagogically glib. The play's structure also requires accurately revealing linking of key words or concepts—above all *anankē* ("necessity") and its numerous synonyms, but also *kallos* ("beauty") and the theatrically crucial language of barbarism and bestialization. Even for a dramatist of such thematic concentration as Euripides (pace archaists and Euripidiphobes), the play's governing idea has been rendered with ferocious intensity of development and perfect sureness of scenic language.

To *Hecuba* Janet Lembke brings an impressive range of poetic skills and dramatic experience. Poet, storyteller, naturalist, student of traditional and contemporary culture, she has translated Aeschylus's *Suppliants* and, with C. J. Herington, his *Persians* for Oxford's The Greek Tragedy in New Translations series. In 1973 her *Bronze and Iron: Old Latin Poetry from Its Beginnings to 100 B.C.*, an impressive effort to renew the texture of religious experience in archaic Latin poetry, was published by the University of California Press. In 1989 she published *River Time,* an anecdotal and highly evocative account of life on the banks of North Carolina's Lower Neuse River, depicting lives in step with the aboriginal rhythms of nature. In press is an ambitious new book,

Looking for Eagles: Reflections of a Classical Naturalist, nominally about wildlife in the Lower Neuse, which its author defines as a quest for *kairos,* the place of man in the natural world.

Her collaborator, Harvard-trained Kenneth Reckford, is professor of classics at the University of North Carolina at Chapel Hill, where he has taught for thirty years. Winner of several teaching awards, he was recently named to the Bowman and Gordon Gray Chair for distinguished undergraduate teaching. The author of a critical study, *Horace* (1969), he has also written numerous articles and essays on Virgil, Euripides, Horace, Persius, and T. S. Eliot. His most recent work is the first volume of an ambitious critical study of Aristophanes—*Aristophanes' Old-and-New Comedy: Six Essays in Perspective* (1987), to be followed shortly by the second volume.

Boston   WILLIAM ARROWSMITH AND HERBERT GOLDER

CONTENTS

HECUBA

INTRODUCTION

I

> The day will come when holy Ilium will fall,
> and Priam, and the people of Priam of the good ashen spear.
>
> _(Iliad_ 6, 448–49)

When Polybius, the historian, asked the younger Scipio what he meant in quoting these lines from Homer and weeping, after the last Roman conquest of Carthage, he replied that, as he contemplated human fortune, it was his own country, Rome, for which he felt afraid.

This probably apocryphal story _(Polybius 38, 22)_ illustrates the spirit of Roman _humanitas,_ which was nourished on Greek poetry, art, and philosophy. It goes well with Virgil's _Aeneid,_ where "Troy" stands for all defeated peoples, all nations and ages that must fall so that others may rise; and it stands, too, for each individual's childhood, which he or she is compelled to outgrow. The lament for lost Troy becomes universal, like the Hebrew exiles' lament for lost Jerusalem ("If I forget you, Jerusalem, . . ."), except that they will return in time to rebuild Jerusalem, but Troy, once razed to the ground, will never be rebuilt.

Virgil's account of the fall of Troy derives its spirit (though not its content) from Homer, as well as from Greek tragedy. It was Homer who gave the defeated Trojans as much admiration and sympathy as the Greek victors. Scipio quoted from Hector's meeting with Andromache in _Iliad_ 6. She begs him not to reenter the battle, reminding him of her dependence—and Troy's—on his living valor. And he acknowledges this. He realizes that Troy will fall some day. He feels pity for Priam, for Hecuba, and for his brothers, who will be killed, but most of all for her:

> . . . when one of the Achaeans clad in bronze
> takes you away in tears, your day of freedom finished;
> in Argos you might then weave at another woman's bidding,

> or else you might fetch water from a distant spring,
> against your will. Compulsion will weigh you down. . . .
>
> *(Iliad* 6, 454–58)

All this Hector sees. Yet he rejects his wife's plea, takes up his helmet, reenters the war, and eventually is killed. The *Iliad* ends with mourning and funeral preparations, yet it concludes on a quiet, reassuring note. For the violence of human passions, of fighting and killing, is balanced for Homer and for his hearers by the beauty of noble actions, by the order and regularity of nature, by human understanding (which transcends national borders, as when the old king, Priam, enters Achilles' tent), and by the loveliness of song and its enduring commemoration of what is good, noble, and beautiful in human life.

Fifth-century tragedians drew on Homer, on the "epic cycle" (now mostly lost), and on narrative lyric poetry for the stories of the Trojan War, going back to the birth of Helen, or her abduction by Paris, or to Agamemnon's sacrifice of his daughter Iphigenia (so that the winds might blow and the Greek army sail to Troy), and forward to the return of the Greek victors and the aftershocks of the war in their homelands—most notably the murder of Agamemnon by Clytemnestra and the subsequent agonies of his house. Still other poems portrayed the death throes of Troy itself. Priam is killed at the altar by Neoptolemus, Achilles' violent son. Hector's child, Astyanax, is taken from Andromache's arms and hurled from the walls of Troy by Neoptolemus or, in other versions, killed by Odysseus after the capture of the city. Priam's daughter, the virgin Polyxena, is sacrificed at Achilles' tomb; he may have desired her in life (the story is unclear), so now his ghost demands her blood. Other Trojan women are led away into slavery. Cassandra, Apollo's never-believed prophetess, becomes Agamemnon's concubine. Andromache must go with Neoptolemus. And Hecuba, the aged queen, will be Odysseus's slave—or as such, at least, was she originally intended.

Simone Weil described the *Iliad* as "the poem of force."[1] Her picture of a blind, mechanical necessity beating down on the heads of helpless humans does not exactly suit Homer, but it does suit Euripides. His best-known Trojan play is the *Trojan Women,* performed in 415 B.C. It centers on Hecuba's increasing grief and bitterness as she experiences the madness of Cassandra, the desolation of Andromache, and (in an ironic, almost farcical, scene) the easy survival of Helen, the cause of all this

---

1. Simone Weil, *La Source Grecque* (Paris, 1952), p. 9.

misery, still beautiful, still unrepentant. I have seen hardened individuals weeping during this play, as well as at a performance of Euripides' *Iphigenia at Aulis,* which was revived, with striking timeliness, during the Vietnamese War.

Euripides' *Hecuba,* dating from 425 or 424 B.C., is less well known, yet it has remained a perennial favorite. It was revived on the Greek stage, adapted for Roman audiences, and read in Byzantine schools and Renaissance libraries. Its story of Hecuba's suffering and revenge is so simple that any schoolchild can understand it. Yet it also speaks to the complexities of human character and destiny, as these were captured in a moment in time no less confusing and dangerous than our own; and it speaks of things that bring to our minds and hearts not only a sense of pity, as Homer's Troy could do, but also sheer terror.

II

The scene is Thrace. At the Thracian Chersonese, a small promontory across from Troy, the Greek army pauses on its return voyage. There, as we learn, the boy Polydorus has been murdered secretly by his host, the Thracian king Polymestor, for gold; there, too, Achilles' ghost has appeared above his own burial mound, demanding Polyxena's sacrifice.

To Euripides' Athenian audience, Thrace was a wild northern region inhabited by barbarians, where all manner of uncivilized behavior might be expected. At the same time, the coastal cities of Thrace were a rich, vital, and vulnerable part of the Athenian Empire. The Thracian Chersonese in the northeast had been colonized by Athenians in the sixth century B.C. and was wrested from Persian control after the Second Persian War (480–479 B.C.). It had rich plains; it helped control the corn route from the Black Sea. Of more immediate concern, Athens needed to protect tribute-paying cities farther west in the Thracian Chalcidice. The revolt of one of these, Potidaea, with Corinthian support, was a direct cause of the Peloponnesian War, the lengthy, costly struggle of Greek against Greek (431–404 B.C.). The Athenians, whose anxieties mounted proportionate to their sphere of influence, looked for help wherever they could find it. They made short-lived alliances with such northern kings as Perdiccas II of Macedon (who proved to be an unusually treacherous ally) and Sitalces of Thrace. Both sides were cynical; both were disappointed; it is hard to say who exploited whom. In his *Acharnians* of 425 B.C. Aristophanes satirizes Athenian hopes for Thracian (and Persian) aid. Sitalces, it seems, has sent some Odomantian soldiers, monstrous and crude barbarians, who are presented to the assembly and subsequently steal the comic hero's garlic. A hilarious scene, it shows what many Athenians—including Aristophanes—must have felt, namely, that those Thracian "allies" were a murderous horde, far more troublesome and dangerous than their aid could possibly be worth.

Euripides, writing his *Hecuba* perhaps that same spring, must have asked himself the same questions as Aristophanes. Was it really necessary to deal with Thracian kings? And where, in the end, would all these involvements lead? Poets are not necessarily prophets, and Euripides could not have foreseen the event of 413 B.C., when a band of Thracian soldiers (intended to support the Athenians in Sicily, but arriving too late to sail) gave what help they could, sacking a Boeotian town. As Thucydides tells it,

The Thracians burst into Mycalessus, sacking the houses and temples, and butchered the inhabitants, sparing neither the young nor the old, but methodically killing everyone they met, women and children alike, and even the farm animals and every living thing they saw. For the Thracian race, like all the most bloodthirsty barbarians, are always particularly bloodthirsty when everything is going their own way. So now there was confusion on all sides and death in every shape and form. Among other things, they broke into a boys' school, the largest in the place, into which the children had just entered, and killed every one of them. Thus disaster fell upon the entire city, a disaster more complete than any, more sudden and more horrible.

> (Thucydides, *History of the Peloponnesian War,*
> VII, 29; trans. Rex Warner)

But Euripides scarcely needed to exercise prophetic powers or, indeed, to look to Thrace in order to realize what a world war meant and would mean. By 426 B.C. the exhausting war had dragged on inconclusively for five years. Not merely fighting and killing but plague, frustration, uprooting of families from the country and crowding in the city, scarcity of food, inflation, corruption, and political factionalism and demagoguery had long since disrupted civilized life and embittered the Athenians' normally bright and generous spirit. The year 427 B.C. was especially violent. That spring and summer the Athenians almost annihilated a rebellious ally, Mytilene; the Spartans betrayed an old and admired ally, Plataea, to the jealousy and hatred of the Thebans; and in Corcyra two rival factions, abetted in turn by Corinth and by Athens, plunged into a bloodbath of mutual destruction and revenge. Thucydides makes Corcyra an object lesson in wartime demoralization, when passions run riot, no longer controlled by reason or loyalty, let alone by traditional morality, decency, or fairness. All this happened far from Athens, to the west. Yet an Athenian fleet was anchored in the harbor at Corcyra while the democrats murdered their public and private enemies. Morally as well as physically, the Athenians were there.

What does it mean, then, when Euripides brings us from Troy to Thrace, along with Agamemnon's victorious Greek officers and soldiers and their Trojan slaves? Thrace is a wild and savage world that has never been tamed by civilization. It is also the homeland of Dionysus, the half-tamed god of abandon at whose spring festivals comedies and tragedies were performed. It all seems so primitive and distant, yet Euripides' Thrace, like Conrad's deepest Africa, becomes a "heart of darkness" in which civilized people are strangely and horribly involved.

And horror is precisely where the play begins. A slight, youthful figure comes onstage. He is Polydorus, he tells us, the son of Hecuba and Priam. During the war his father entrusted him and his treasure for safekeeping to their guest-friend (*xenos*) Polymestor, the Thracian king, but when Troy fell Polymestor violated the most sacred bonds of trust. He killed the boy for his gold and threw the body into the sea. Yet things will turn out well, Polydorus says, for his body will be washed ashore and revealed to his mother, Hecuba, just after his sister, Polyxena, is sacrificed to Achilles' ghost near this very same Thracian shore. So this nice, simple ghost will get the burial he deserves. The gods of the underworld have been kind to him. To Hecuba, who now enters, terrified by dreams, the gods will be less kind.

III

The play falls into two halves—almost into two plays. The first might be called "Polyxena's Sacrifice," and the second "Hecuba's Revenge."

The first begins, after the ghost scene, with Hecuba's emergence from the central tent. Although her frightful dream of wolf rending fawn alludes to Polydorus's murder, the chorus focuses both Hecuba's attention and ours on the impending sacrifice of Polyxena. Achilles' ghost demanded it and the Greek army consented. The report of their debate, with all its politicking, moves the sphere of action further from Homer's noble world and closer to everyday realities at Athens. Polyxena, called out of the tent by Hecuba, who laments with her, exudes an old-fashioned nobility; she speaks and moves as a Trojan (and Homeric) princess ought. The Odysseus, however, who comes with soldiers to take her is not Homer's wise and compassionate hero but a coldly rational officer and politician who serves necessity and expects others to do the same: "Even in bad times it's prudent/to use common sense" (ll. 244–45). Good advice, for him, is what works best at the moment. When Hecuba pleads with him to save Polyxena—appealing to such traditional values as decency, fairness, personal gratitude, and respect for suppliants—he counters her plea, as a sophist-trained orator might in 420 B.C., with high-sounding phrases and arguments, very much like Hecuba's yet somehow ringing hollow. Now it is Polyxena's turn, but she will not plead. She will die free, not live the life of a slave. She departs, untouched and free, with Odysseus's soldiers. After the chorus sings a song of exile and of lingering hope, a messenger, the compassionate Talthybius, comes to inform Hecuba of her daughter's death. The queen grieves but admires Polyxena's enduring nobility. Sending a serving-woman to fetch seawater to bathe the corpse, Hecuba reenters the central tent, leaving the stage empty, as if at the end of a play.

Then, after a brief choral ode on the sorrows of the Trojan War (and of all wars), the second part begins. The servingwoman returns, a corpse is carried onstage, and Hecuba reemerges to learn the worst. Her agony reaches its peak as she discovers not Polyxena's body but her murdered boy's. With this blow her last hope is gone. But after a few cries of utter pain, she turns to action with renewed decisiveness and vigor. She pleads with Agamemnon to assist her in her desire for revenge. This time her determination carries the day, for Agamemnon is a weak-willed man and an indecisive general, anxious to preserve his image before the world. He agrees to lend passive support to Hecuba. For her that is enough. Like an effective general, she takes charge of the situation. With her women's help, she lures Polymestor to the camp and into the prisoners' tent, kills his two young children, and puts out his eyes. The smiling villain, the Thracian king, is reduced to a howling, helpless beast. Agamemnon is "shocked" by these events. Presiding over a mockery of a trial, he passes judgment against Polymestor, who then prophesies disaster for all concerned. As soldiers and slaves prepare to sail for Greece (for the winds are blowing again), the play ends.

The play's two halves differ in tone and pace. In the first part, which centers on fear, grief, and loss, things are still done slowly, deliberately, with a certain dignity and grace. It might almost be a tragedy by Sophocles. In the second part excitement builds and events occur rapidly. The audience will be caught up in the excitement, wanting Hecuba to win, hissing the villain Polymestor—and finding the end result appalling. The scenes involving Polymestor are pure black comedy. The trial scene is a parody of tragic resolution. The finale is unsettling. It is, unmistakably, a play by Euripides.

But the play's two halves are unified through plot, character development, and metaphorical and thematic statement. Most obviously, Polydorus's ghost foretells what will happen; the discovery of his body, confidently anticipated by him, destroys what is left of Hecuba's spirit. Her passion for revenge, on the other hand, arises naturally enough from her grief and loneliness and eventually supplants it. Like that other Euripidean heroine, Medea, she moves relentlessly forward to an almost demonic victory over her enemies that is, at the same time, a measure of her defeat as a person, her inward dehumanization.

Hecuba's bearing controls the play, marking the stages of action and meaning. At first her movements convey a sense of weakness coupled with inner effort and half-hearted resolution. She walks slowly onstage, leaning on a staff, supported by attendants; she kneels painfully to clasp Odysseus's knees in supplication and rises up again to confront him; she collapses to the ground, torn from her daughter, and lies there like a corpse; and yet, stirred by Talthybius's kindness and decency, she rises up once more and walks with dignity. This was the queen of Troy. In the second part, we expect her to collapse, but she does not. She stiffens. She speaks and moves with resolution. No need for measure now, nor dignity; what matters is command. Hecuba moves quickly, perhaps without her staff. She gives orders; she controls events, though they are meant to destroy, not save; she is a queen again, though not a Trojan queen, and not for long.

The play's two halves are now one. It portrays Hecuba's suffering and her revenge, the one following from the other as lightning breaks from storm clouds (a metaphor used by Euripides to describe Medea's anger). It also portrays a fall from grace, from decency, from the innocence and nobility of the "Trojan" or Homeric world. The play is not just about Hecuba's fall, for what she learns as a result of her suffering and from "instructors" like Odysseus and Polymestor is that she lives in a godforsaken world where chance and harsh necessity prevail and where no one (general, victor, king) is truly free. Polyxena died free, like a Trojan princess, while she still could. Hecuba lives on, a broken spirit in a shattered world.

IV

As befits her upbringing, Polyxena dies a free, noble, even beautiful death; but if she had lived on, she reasons in order to console her mother, she would have to endure the compulsions of slavery:

> I might chance, too, on a brutal master
> who'd haggle and trade silver coins for me—

sister to Hector and the many others,
and he'd constrain me to his needs—grind corn, make bread,
sweep dirt from his house, stand at the loom,
each day know grief. He'll force constraint on me.
And a slave, bought who knows where, will foul
my bed that was reserved for kings.

(ll. 386–93)

We are reminded of Homer again, of Hector's tender words to Andromache. But Euripides' picture of slavery is much harsher. It does not
include drawing water from some lovely Greek spring (an image to be
recalled shortly by Euripides' still hopeful chorus). It ends with a brutal
rape—the negation of all that Polyxena has been and chooses to be.

Her instinct is right—more than she realizes—when she advises her
mother that to die is sometimes better than to live:

. . . But agree that I should
die before my dignity is made ugly by shame.
One not accustomed to the taste of cruelty
endures it but bends her neck to the yoke of anguish.
Dying would be better luck than living,
for life without moral beauty inflicts endless pain.

(ll. 400–405)

The Greek word *kalos* here used by Polyxena means "beautiful," "fine,"
and "noble." In Euripides' time it referred not just to physical beauty but
also, by an easy and common transference, to moral beauty and grace
(much as we still say "that was a beautiful thing to do" or "she's a
beautiful person"). The "life without moral beauty" rejected by Polyxena is also life without nobility, grace, or honor. Opposed to *kalos* and
contrasted with it throughout the play is *aischros,* meaning "ugly,"
"foul," "ignoble," or "shameful." In the traditional Greek view, even
ignoble actions carried out under compulsion are *felt* to be ugly and to
infect the doer with ugliness, which is why Talthybius later asserts that
he "would rather/die than let chance plunge me/in the ugliness of
shame" (ll. 525–27). Polyxena, then, not only dies beautifully but in
dying also escapes an ugly life, the despoiling of her Trojan nobility. At
that moment in the messenger's report when she offers herself freely to
Neoptolemus's sacrificial knife, baring her "breasts that gleamed like a
statue's/carved to honor the gods . . ." (ll. 593–94), her physical and
moral beauty seem caught up and immortalized. We think of the figures
on Keats's Grecian urn, or of Sophocles's unyielding heroes and heroines, who, even in the act of dying, defy time and change. Their will
and sense of self live on unstained.

Hecuba grieves for Polyxena's death, but she is consoled by the beauty, decency, and nobility of that death, as reported by Talthybius. And this sense of consolation precludes excessive grief. Polyxena had been Hecuba's prop and support, like the staff she leans upon: "She is my better self, my consolation, / my country, nurse, staff, guide." (ll. 301–2). Now all that support is withdrawn. Yet for a brief time the queen is still upheld inwardly by the image of her daughter's nobility, which reflects her own. So she can, for now, continue.

In a strangely reflective and self-conscious speech, Hecuba muses on the nature of human nobility. Many critics, since ancient times, have found her remarks peripheral, but they hold an ironic central place in the play's thematic development. For Hecuba, musing on her daughter's grace under compulsion, also dwells on what seems a paradox: In human nature, inborn nobility endures, whereas in the fields good soil cannot always guarantee good results, since plants depend on such external factors as sunlight, rain, and human attentiveness for their sustenance and growth. But Hecuba's paradox is as unstable as the old aristocratic values on which it is based. Its very language indicates that it cannot hold up. Only in the perfection of sculpture, music, or death can human virtue and nobility remain constant. It may be that for the living virtue can be taught as well as inherited (this was a hotly debated subject in Euripides' own time). What matters to Euripides in this play, as in many others, is that virtue can be *untaught,* good character corrupted, and nobility destroyed. And this is what happens to Hecuba in the ugly and shameful sequel. She outlives her daughter and her better self. She falls into a state of slavery and evil. If her glowing words on nobility serve as a kind of funeral oration for Polyxena, they are also appropriate for the Trojan queen, for Homer's Hecuba, who will shortly fade from sight.

V

There is no question that we are all sympathetic to Hecuba's cause after she discovers the mutilated body of her son. We want her revenge to succeed and it does. After receiving so many orders, Hecuba takes command; after suffering so much horror, she inflicts it; after trusting, without avail, in men and gods, she lures the too trusting deceiver Polymestor to his ruin. Revenge is all she wants now, and it is what she gets. And we, the audience, are caught up vicariously in the wild and bloody exultation of her revenge, as in a Dionysian revel where the god's maddened votaries, his maenads, tear their animal (or human) victim limb from limb.

As is often the case, it is the chorus, occupying an intermediate position between actors and audience, that sets the tone as their mood turns from grief and sympathy to anger. Their first choral ode is a lament over their state of exile. They wonder, still hopeful, in what land they might be destined to serve. Perhaps it will be a holy land where the gods are honored. The second ode, harsh and brief, speaks of necessary toil and of the fateful union of Paris and Helen. It ends with the image of a bloody fingernail rending the cheek's flesh in an act of universal mourning. But the third ode—saddest and most beautiful of all in its description of Troy's last night of happiness and ruin—ends in a curse against Helen and Paris and the wish that she may never return home again. The earlier compassionate ending is no more. Now, just prior to Polymestor's entrance with his two children, the uprooted women pray that their enemy may be uprooted like themselves. We should recall the psalm that begins:

> By the rivers of Babylon
> there we sat and wept,
> remembering Sion,

but ends,

> O Babylon, destroyer,
> he is happy who repays you
> the ills you brought on us.
> He shall seize and shall dash
> your children on the rock!

The anger of the Trojan women rouses us to further complicity in Hecuba's revenge.

Prior to the choral ode, as Hecuba pleads with Agamemnon for support, we are excited by the force of her argument and the will with which she manages to overbear the Greek commander. How much ought we to realize that her new power, her energy of mind and will, springs from disillusionment and from despair? She repeats the old, familiar arguments—the appeal to the gods, to custom and law (*nomos*), to justice—but now she uses them as Odysseus himself had done, playing a game of persuasion utilizing counters with no real validity of their own. Indeed, as she intimates (her language here is crafty and ambiguous), the only real divinity remaining is the goddess Persuasion, or the tongue's power to obtain what the will requires. Master the art of persuasion and you will have (reading between the lines) a god's power in a godforsaken world. Since the old values of loyalty, trust, honor, decency, and fair play have vanished into thin air, other things have

INTRODUCTION

taken their place; in pursuing your goal—be it wealth or power or revenge—it is now permissible to use any means that comes to hand. Reason itself and rational discourse have been debased to serve this end, as has sex. With the quick insight born of cunning and desperation, Hecuba realizes that sex is real to Agamemnon, though honor and decency are not. She reminds him of the happy nights he has spent hugging Cassandra and demands "what thanks, what fee" (l. 875) she will get for these. The request is shocking. Nothing could contrast more strongly with the modesty of Polyxena's life and death. But it is granted, and Agamemnon agrees, to comply tacitly with Hecuba's act of revenge, paying lip service to the gods, justice, and the rest. That clears her way, and she proceeds from there.

We have begun, I think, to perceive a coarsening in Hecuba's words, gestures, and actions that will become more apparent later on. For now, her change of heart is captured precisely in a brief but passionate statement. When Agamemnon asks, with extraordinary carelessness,

> What do you crave? Freedom?
> That's easy.

she quickly responds,

> No, no! Revenge on criminals,
> and I'll be slave for all my days to come.
> (ll. 794–97)

For nobody is truly free. Hecuba sees that now; it is another worthless counter. But she discovers in her slavery a terrible new freedom and power, sensing that it is her destiny to track down her enemy as a hound might a wolf, and to rend him with bloody nails.

Polymestor is lured, caught, and rent. However much we may have desired his punishment in the form of torture or death, his actual reappearance is horrifying; the king has been reduced to a frenzied animal lurching to and fro in search of human flesh. Moreover, his two dead children are carried silently onstage and laid upon the ground, as Polydorus's body had been earlier. We had just seen them, alive and cheerful, innocent of their father's treachery. Two dead boys for one. It is a spectacle not of justice carried out, of what we might reasonably and fairly have hoped for, but of human atrocity.

Nor does the final courtroom scene produce anything like real justice. It is, rather, like the great mistrials in the fiction of Stendhal, Dostoievski, or Kafka, a parody of all that law and justice were meant to be. The judge, Agamemnon, is prejudiced and corrupt. (We know what he was bribed with.) The plaintiff, Polymestor, is easily refuted, though less on moral grounds than of being an unreliable ally of the Greeks. The debate, for Agamemnon, is a political one, and Polymestor is of no further use to him, so Hecuba wins hands down. Now the Greek army can go about its business of returning home.

Yet there is more to be said, and Polymestor, of all people, says it. In place of the god who often appears at the end of a Greek tragedy to establish some memorial rite or to announce the restoration of the social and political order, we are surprised to hear the blinded, half-crazed Polymestor speaking with prophetic insight about the future. He foretells how Hecuba will be transformed into a fiery-eyed dog, plunging from the ship's mast into the sea; the promontory of Cynossema, "bitch's rock," will be her memorial. Hecuba is only slightly shocked, for she has won her revenge, and the prophesied transformation and suicide is only the outward, visible sign of an inner transformation—or dehumanization—that has been taking place all along. But Polymestor goes on, foretelling still other disasters. Cassandra will be killed, and Agamemnon will be murdered by his wife. What awaits the king, the Greek victor (and the audience knows it) is bloody slaughter. His answer is to muzzle the prophet. The misfortunes of the Greeks can be related in other plays. Agamemnon prays for a good return, for release from toil. The winds are blowing at last. The fleet can sail. The Trojan women make ready for their bondage in Greece, from which there is now "no escape."

VI

It is one thing to become demoralized as a result of one's own excessive suffering, but quite another to confront a demoralized world, one in which, as Polymestor says, "Nothing at all can be trusted" (l. 1009). He ought to know. A man who has broken the most sacred ties of honor, decency, and guest-friendship, he is even now toying with his victim's mother—and she with him. Ironically, Polymestor proves too trusting; he thinks that the women's tents are safe. And he is caught like a savage beast or a barbarian who is finally punished for his uncivilized behavior. As Agamemnon puts it, displaying a Greek consciousness of superiority, "Among *your* people, perhaps it's easy / to murder guests. / To us, the Greeks, this deed is ugly in its shame" (ll. 1340–42). Did the Athenian audience applaud? They must have enjoyed the defeat and humiliation of the villain. It is comforting to see justice meted out. And Thrace, where these ugly events occurred, must have seemed reassuringly remote from Athens. Or did it?

As Euripides was writing *Hecuba,* Athens was not only active in

Thrace but was also engaged in a long, demoralizing war that pitted Greek against Greek. When Thucydides describes the brutality of events at Corcyra and the breakdown of all basic values—religious, moral, familial, and even of reason itself as it is embodied in meaningful discourse, when he laments the passing of that old-time spirit of simplicity and openness "to which nobility most largely contributes" (*History of the Peloponnesian War*, III, 83. 1) (we think of Polyxena) that "was laughed down and altogether disappeared" (III, 83. 1); we begin to wonder whether it is war and civil strife that are the exception, destroying normal life, or whether it is that normal, civilized, "Athenian" life itself that constitutes the exception to the usual chaos.

Nor can we say that trust in the gods or in an underlying moral code are simply overwhelmed by the extreme nature of war. Modern thought can also induce a metaphysical crisis of meaning and belief, and to a keen observer like Euripides it was doing just that in Athens well before the Peloponnesian War broke out. Physics and astronomy; empirical medicine; comparative ethnography; naturalistic anthropology; the new rhetorical exercises in conceptual analysis, definition, and argumentation—all these ongoing developments undermined people's blind confidence in the workings of divine and human law and in the authority of accepted codes of behavior. What replaced these values for some was pride in science and technology, in the ascent of man. It seemed a grand success story, a panoramic view of human progress from primitive beginnings, through the gradual, experimental, and self-taught mastery of tools and methods, to the building of towns and cultures and advanced civilizations. All this was admirable, but the price was a new sense of the precariousness of laws, customs, institutions, and rational discourse. Could these things be waived on occasion? Could they be manipulated by clever people who perceived themselves to be above the law? Certainly, they could collapse under sufficient pressure—and not merely the pressure of war. When the plague invaded Athens in 430–429 B.C. and no effective remedy could be found, not even the most sacred laws— for example, those of burial—were able to withstand the weight of human despair. And this happened not in savage or mythic Thrace but in Athens a mere five years before Euripides' *Hecuba* was staged.

Viewed in this light, one can understand how Hecuba's demoralization parallels her discovery of a demoralized world. Odysseus and Polymestor are her teachers or, more precisely her "un-teachers." Odysseus, deaf to Hecuba's pleas, blind to her as a real person, illustrates how old-fashioned values like decency, honor, and gratitude may be laughed at and may disappear altogether. Polyxena's actions in preparation for her impending death mirror these golden values of nobility at their best and brightest, but the discovery of Polydorus's little mutilated body simply annihilates them both for Hecuba and for the world. From that point on, Hecuba's passionate energy and her sure-footed movement toward revenge spring from a newfound, cynical, even nihilistic assurance that values do not count. The gods, law, honor, justice—all are mere words, though words that retain some half-persuasive force. Other forces are more real; greed, lust, and persuasion can be made to serve revenge. What rules the world, finally, is neither god nor law but incalculable chance (*tychê*). In such a world, there is no privileged space for human dignity, nor even for human freedom. Everyone, as Hecuba says, is equally a slave. That being so, one must grapple like a slave for what one can.

When we, the audience, find ourselves applauding Agamemnon's verdict against the barbarian Polymestor, we seem to be cooperating, like Agamemnon in Thrace or the Athenians at Corcyra, with destructive passions far beyond our understanding or control. For the play appears to be a mockery of justice and order. In the gods' absence, Hecuba devises her own brand of justice; Agamemnon makes his; Clytemnestra will make hers. There is no order, no morality, in this chance-ruled universe. We do not even have the consolation (if one considers it thus) of seeing dark powers at work, like the witches in *Macbeth,* making the clouding of reason and will more understandable. In Euripides' *Hippolytus* there is Aphrodite; in his *Bacchae* there is Dionysus. *Hecuba* lacks even amoral gods. There are ghosts, certainly, but they act mainly as catalysts. Behind the scene there is only chance and blind necessity. Perhaps this mood is best caught in the image of the winds that suddenly stop blowing, forcing the Greek army to be detained in Thrace, and reappear again at the play's end—but only after Hecuba has won her revenge. What the winds of fortune grant in this play is time not for good but for evil; and that, in a blind universe, is as close as Euripides lets us come to sensing a dark power at work.

VII

We come, then, to the emotions of pity and fear, which Aristotle says are purged, or clarified, by experiencing painful events represented on the stage. As we read *Hecuba,* the words seem inadequate. Pity is what we feel for noble people who have fallen into misfortune—for Homer's Trojan king and queen, whose country is invaded, whose children are slain, and who slide from prosperity to ruin as the gods' favor deserts them; or we might feel pity for Polyxena, dying so young and still a virgin;

or for the Trojan women, bundled off into slavery in distant lands. For Hecuba pity seems inadequate as she falls into a slavery of the soul, into what Simone Weil has described as *malheur,* as opposed to mere *douleur:* "In the realm of suffering, affliction is something apart, specific, and irreducible. It is quite a different thing from simple suffering. It takes possession of the soul and marks it through and through with its own particular mark, the mark of slavery. . . ."[2] Euripides' Hecuba exemplifies the worst possible fate that can happen to human beings; it is appalling, bound up with terror. Fear, moreover, is too weak a word for the impact of these events. Simple fear is what we feel when the ghost appears, when Hecuba describes her dream, when we struggle (with her) against the realization that Polyxena will have to be sacrificed. These fears are confirmed—and resolved—as the play's action unfolds. We experience terror, though, at the possibility that we and the people we love might suffer what Hecuba suffers; and we feel terror at that other possibility, namely, that the world we have come to know and trust—the world of Troy, of Athens, of Western civilization—might suddenly metamorphose into Thrace or, rather, might reveal itself as the world of blind, mechanical necessity that Weil has described so well:

If the mechanism were not blind there would not be any affliction. Affliction is anonymous before all things; it deprives its victims of their personality and makes them into things. It is indifferent; and it is the coldness of this indifference—a metallic coldness—that freezes all those it touches right to the depths of their souls. . . .

Human crime, which is the cause of most affliction, is part of blind necessity, because criminals do not know what they are doing.[3]

There is compassion in these lines even for war criminals. There is also a chillling horror of the godforsaken world that might, but for God's grace, be our own.

Of course, there have always been ways of evading the full impact of tragic pity and terror. One way is to claim, rather like Agamemnon, that it happened in Thrace, that only barbarians act like animals. This is, as I have suggested, to miss the point. Some years ago, after a performance of William Alfred's *Hogan's Goat,* which is set in late nineteenth-century Brooklyn, I heard one spectator say to another, "How lucky this sort of thing doesn't happen today," which, in its way, recalls the Victorian lady's comment on *Antony and Cleopatra:* "How unlike, how very unlike, the home life of our own dear Queen!"

2. Simone Weil, *Waiting For God,* trans. Emma Craufurd. (New York, 1951), p. 117.
3. Ibid., p. 125.

There is also the use of esthetic distancing as a mode of evasion. The choral odes, in particular, are a delight to read and must have seemed even more beautiful when they were sung and danced to music by a well-trained chorus. These odes provide emotional variety and relief, qualities easily overlooked today. They are often mistakenly viewed—especially in Euripides' later tragedies—as escapist pieces, distractions from the main tragic event. In *Hecuba,* it is rather Euripides' heightened sense of the fragility of all things good and beautiful that leads him to express, in new and strange ways, the loveliness of ordinary life—"the home life," we might say, "of our own dear Queen!"—and the pain and sorrow of losing it. There is an extraordinarily touching moment in the third ode when the young Trojan wife makes herself ready for bed: "I was arranging my hair, / binding it up in ribbons for the night, / and a golden mirror's endless sunlight / held my gaze" (ll. 977–80). It is an ordinary moment, yet an intensely precious one, for the next moment will bring confusion and sudden death; the wife, her husband newly slain, will find herself being carried off into exile, looking back sadly to Troy. To take another example, in the first ode the chorus consoles itself in the face of slavery and exile with the wistful hope that it might be taken to places of physical and spiritual beauty—to the holy isle of Delos, perhaps, or to Athens, where its citizens join in the lovely Panathenaic ceremonies. The sense of beauty, of ceremony, of worship of the gods is comforting. (We might recall that the presentation of Greek tragedies was only one part of the Athenian festival of Dionysus, god of wine and release.) But the feeling of consolation fades as the play unfolds, even as the feeling of lost happiness grows more passionate and intense.

The realization of life's fragility can also result in a sense of compassion that overrides boundaries and reaches out to one's enemies. In the second ode, the chorus sings of how ". . . laments also rise / by the banks of a sunlit Greek river / where a Spartan girl cries alone in her room" (ll. 685–87). It is Homeric and "Trojan," this awareness that the Greeks experience sadness, too. But the Spartan girl is, after all, a representative of the enemy. In an Athenian theater, before thousands of angry and frustrated Athenians, writing (and speaking) these lines took courage. Euripides was a cosmopolitan, but he was no less patriotic on that account. His sense of the beauty and fragility of things, which the citizens of all nations experience equally since they are all human beings, made him love his own Athenian homeland all the more passionately, not for its glory, or even for its advanced civilization, but because (as Scipio perceived at Carthage) that glory and that advanced civilization could so easily be destroyed.

VIII

Much that I have said will not seem especially new or surprising to many classical scholars, for Euripides' *Hecuba* is not a problem play. Most twentieth-century criticism is sane, balanced, and to the point. I am indebted, among others, to the work of Abrahamson, Conacher, Daitz, Garzya, Grube, Kirkwood, Luschnig, Matthaei, Pohlenz, and especially that of Jacqueline de Romilly. The best pages written on *Hecuba* are still those of William Arrowsmith in The University of Chicago Press series of translations (now available in a Modern Library edition). I have also seen, and been stimulated by, unpublished writings by Martha Nussbaum and Ann Michelini, and have made extensive use of my own somewhat unbalanced lecture entitled "Concepts of Demoralization in Euripides' *Hecuba*," which was presented in March 1977 at a Euripides symposium held at Duke University.[4] Alice Radin provided me with much advice and information regarding the character of Polyxena.

I referred to my lecture as "somewhat unbalanced" because I focused my attention exclusively on a few key passages. In order to make original observations the critic must often do this; but in doing so he or she may obstruct the play's flow, obscure its emotional impact, or become too preoccupied with the printed text. The Oxford University Press series "The Greek Tragedy in New Translations" compensates the critic for all this. There is the challenge of writing for nonspecialists (I almost wrote "for a live audience"). There is the pleasure, for one who can read Greek, of being yoked together with a poet who can write *English,* who can breathe life and movement into the printed page. As companion spirits, Janet Lembke and I found ourselves asking the same basic questions of the text: what is happening here, and what does it mean? We felt, with equal passion, that the play *moved* (esthetically, dramatically, emotionally) and that a live audience should and would be moved by it. At the same time, Janet has conveyed—and helped me to realize—the crisp, neat lines, the conciseness and power of Euripides' play.

We owe much to William Arrowsmith, who harnessed this particular chariot and set the pace. He has been a model of clear thinking, clear writing, and the confrontation of what he has called "turbulence" in Greek drama. I owe a similar yet stronger and older debt to the late Robert A. Brooks. He was my teacher, my predecessor (in several ways)

---

4. Papers presented at this symposium will be published shortly by Duke University Press under the title *Directions in Euripidean Criticism,* to be edited by Peter Burian, the organizer of the symposium.

in this series, and the father-in-law I never had. For my part, I wish to dedicate this effort to Rab and Jane, in thanks for their enduring generosity to my wife, Mary, and to me.

Chapel Hill, N.C.   K.J.R.
February 1984

TRANSLATOR'S NOTE

One of the principles underlying Oxford's series "The Greek Tragedy in New Translations" is that the latter be performable. This is a praiseworthy and necessary aim, but how can it be achieved? The answer lies, I believe, in testing through performance. Plays exist only secondarily as literature. Like music and dance, they are, first and foremost, part of the performing arts.

For me, translating Greek tragedy begins in silence. The Greek words are strung across the pages like formidably precise strands of barbed wire. They hold neither music nor movement. But gradually the mind limbers and the tongue gains a stumbling facility for turning separate letters into sounds, for piling those sounds up to form whole words and lines. Patterns emerge; the rhythms begin to be heard; the work of translation begins.

That work involves finding the English words and rhythms that most readily recreate the sense of the original play. By sense, I mean both verbal and affective content. On the one hand, the words chosen should be as faithful as possible to literal meaning. On the other, they must sing, shout, whisper, march, hesitate, rise and fall in ways that suggest the nonverbal elements of the original—its meters, its actions and dramatic pace, its tug at the emotions. Making such choices calls for much scribbling and muttering; the results fill reams of paper.

The translator's mind becomes a stage. What is an audience supposed to *see?* Characters enter, speak, and exit. The chorus sings and dances. The play is tried out in a mind's eye version of the classical Athenian theater, complete with musical accompaniment, stage building, entrance passages, and seating for at least ten thousand people. The imagination also mounts the play in more contemporary settings, including a proscenium stage or a theater-in-the-round.

Decisions are made. English simulacra of speech, chant, and song are transcribed onto paper. Stage directions are inferred from hints supplied in the characters' words, for the Greek text contains no directions. A script comes into being, but silence still threatens, for the script is tentative, a collection of written symbols, an effort that has been played out only in solitary fancy. It can be read, but can it be transferred from page to stage? Is it performable? Is it truly alive?

The worth of a play's translation is demonstrated, I believe, only in the fleeting moment of performance, be it a walk-through with scripts in hand or a full production. At some point the translation-in-progress should—I want to say *must*—be tested for performability: the fit of words in actors' mouths; the meshing of words and actions; the efficiency of the invented directions; the applause or restless fidgeting of an audience. The translator may then make changes, see and hear them enacted, and decide—with the help of others—what to keep, drop, or alter further.

With help: theater is now, and has always been, an intensely cooperative enterprise. In the case of translation, the translator stands in, however inadequately, for the playwright. But the written translation lacks juice; its words can only suggest sound, motion, and spectacle to the lone reader. As a play it has no reality until it finds intermediaries—director and actors—who can perform the ultimate act of translation by breathing life into the script and delivering it directly to an audience. The audience, in turn, plays an active role in testing by providing its own cues to players and director as they transform static script into immediate activity. To be a member of an audience is to participate in a common sensory experience denied the lone reader.

Performance can also suggest, as the page cannot, the vanished elements of the original: music and dance. The surviving Greek tragedies have been compared to libretti that have lost their operas; the plays are seen as texts forever separated from their contexts. This is not quite so, for performance provides context. The actors' voices alone constitute a kind of music, and blocking conveys a sense of choreography. A director may go still further by giving fancy footwork to the chorus and providing live or recorded music as background to lyric passages. The possibilities for embellishment are limited only by their appropriateness to the drama being staged. Such dance and music cannot, of course, reproduce the originals, but they can give the contemporary audience an understanding—remote, perhaps, but an understanding nonetheless—of tragedy's original threefold nature, its intricate braiding of words, music, and dance.

Testing, yes! Chance has granted this version of *Hecuba* just such a trial by performance. Many individuals have contributed their knowledge and encouragement to the work of translation. Chief among them is H. Rick Hite, professor of Theater/Communications and chairman of the Humanities Division at Virginia Wesleyan College. He rallied student actors and put them through their paces on a stage that was in no way imaginary. He summoned an audience. During several performances I could hear the clunkers that had sounded fluent in the scribbling-and-muttering phase; could see the loose ends that had seemed tightly joined; could gauge the audience's attentiveness by its cough-and-rustle quotient. Moreover, performance reveals aspects of a play that are not readily apparent to a reader or to the translator playing out the drama in the mind's eye. For example, in solitude it is easy to forget that Polyxena is onstage during the long dialogue between Hecuba and Odysseus. But the theatergoer knows that she is indeed physically present as her mother pleads for her daughter's life while Odysseus adamantly and arrogantly refuses all mercy. With such insights, the work of revision could begin.

For this testing experience thanks also must go to Bentley Anderson, whose set converted the theater into a tented encampment on the coast of Thrace or any such encampment where the ruinous aftermath of war demands more degradation, more death. Credit must be given to the cast, who willingly tackled difficult, painful material, and in particular to Mary Christine Danner, who played Hecuba with a trained skill not usually found in a collegiate actor. How rewarding to hear her say, "It's been easy to learn my lines."

Even more rewarding has been the opportunity to proceed under the gentle, informed tutelage of Kenneth Reckford, who has always seen *Hecuba* as a play "with possibilities for performance that usually go unrecognized in the reading of a Greek text." Other "Editors' Forewords" to this series have referred to "collaboration between scholar and poet." Collaboration, however, is too impersonal a word to describe our teamwork. Cooperation better describes a dual effort that began auspiciously with Kenneth's firm wish that "we must borrow a stage and an audience after a while." Sometimes wishes do come true.

But before such inspired cooperation could burgeon, an initial decision to undertake a translation had to be made. The impetus behind the decision came from William Arrowsmith. It was he who urged me to abandon Aeschylus and try my hand at Euripides—specifically *Hecuba,* which he himself has translated with commendable performability. And it was he who suggested that Kenneth Reckford be my guide.

The text used is that edited by Stephen G. Daitz (Teubner, 1973). Professor Daitz also gave my ear its first chance to hear the music of the Greek; he has recorded the entire play on tapes that accompany his prose translation (Jeffrey Norton Publishers, 1981). The prose translation helped greatly in resolving several problems of interpretation. Professor Daitz was good enough, as well, to send me a copy of his article "Concepts of Freedom and Slavery in Euripides' *Hecuba*" (*Hermes*, 99, no. 2 [1971]).

Last to be mentioned but far from last in my thoughts as I slowly made my way through the tale of Hecuba's self-enslavement are my daughters, Elisabeth and Hannah, to whom my efforts are dedicated. May their lot be beauty, dignity, and freedom.

Staunton, Va.   J.L.
February 1984

HECUBA

CHARACTERS

GHOST OF POLYDORUS
HECUBA queen of Troy, widow of Priam,
mother of Polydorus and Polyxena
CHORUS of captive Trojan women
POLYXENA daughter of Hecuba
ODYSSEUS Greek commander
TALTHYBIUS the Greeks' herald
SERVING WOMAN Hecuba's attendant
AGAMEMNON Greek commander
POLYMESTOR king of Thrace

Serving women, attendants to Hecuba
Greek soldiers
Two boys, sons of Polymestor
Thracian attendants of Polymestor

Line numbers in the right-hand margin of the text refer to
the English translation only, and the Notes at p. 81 are
keyed to these lines. The bracketed line numbers in the
running headlines refer to the Greek text.

The coast of Thrace. In the background center, AGAMEMNON'S *tent, where* HECUBA *is quartered. On either side, tents housing the captive women.*

The GHOST OF POLYDORUS enters left.

GHOST I come
         out of the pit that hides the dead,
         out of the gate-guarded darkness
  where Hades lives separate from other gods.
  I come,
         Polydorus, Hecuba's son
  and Priam's. My father saw danger—
  our Troy falling under Greek spears.
  Fearful, he smuggled me from Trojan soil
  to Polymestor, his friend in Thrace,   10
  who plants these fertile plains
  and rules a horse-loving people.
  And my father sent me with much secret gold.
  Then, if the walls of Troy should fall,
  his children—those who lived—would not be poor.
  And I was youngest of Priam's sons.
  He smuggled me out, for I was a boy,
  too young to carry heavy shield and lance.

  As long as our boundaries held
  and Troy's towers stood unbroken   20
  and chance blessed my brother Hector's spear,
  how quickly, cared for by my father's friend,
  I grew, like a young tree reaching tall, to be cut.
  For, Troy met ruin. So did Hector's life.
  And my father's hearth was leveled to the ground,
  and there by the godbuilt altar, he fell,
  slaughtered for sacrifice
         by Achilles' murder-stained son.
  My father's friend killed me as I grieved. For gold

he killed me and threw my body in the sea   30
so he could keep that gold within his house.

I lie ashore, I lie in the breaking sea
sucked back, tossed up by waves that surge and lapse,
unwept, unburied.
                        And now, my shell of flesh
left empty, I am only air that flickers
lightly over her I love, my mother Hecuba.
Three days I have hovered—
ever since my helpless mother was landed here
far from Troy on this Thracian soil.   40
And all the Greeks, becalmed with their ships,
are waiting ashore for a fair wind.
For, dead Achilles showed himself above his tomb
to hold back the army of the Greeks
as they plied oars toward home.
He claims my sister Polyxena for his tomb
as the sacrifice he covets, as a last prize.
And it shall come to pass:
He shall not go giftless. His friends will honor him.
Fate leads my sister on this day to her dying.   50

And, two children's two corpses—how closely
my mother shall see them, mine and my doomed sister's.
For I will show myself in surf at a slave's feet
so that my torn flesh shall find its grave.
For the gods below have might, and I have begged them,
Let me claim a tomb, claim the hands of my mother
to bury me. And all, all I have wished for
shall come to pass.

                        Hecuba, grey, old—I must draw back.
She walks from Agamemnon's tent   60
frightened. She dreamed my ghost.

                                                (*moans*)

O mother, sheltered in a royal house and come
to slavery, you know life's harshness now
as once you knew its joy. Some god gives you
ruin equal to the riches lost.

The GHOST *exits left.* HECUBA, *holding a wooden staff,*
enters from AGAMEMNON'S *tent with her serving women.*

HECUBA *(chanting)*
Lead children, lead this old one from her house.
Lead, Trojan women. Raise to her feet
the fellow slave once your lady and queen.
Come, carry me, lead me, lift me
taking my old hand.   70
Lend me your arms bent for a crutch.
And I—let me lean—I will hasten with slow
stiff-ankled steps.

O lightning of Zeus, O dark-brooding Night,
why am I caught up, held captive nightlong
by terrors, ghosts? O Queen below earth,
mother of dreams, black-wingèd dreams,
let me push away nightmares that still possess me—

dreams of the one who found safety in Thrace, my young
son,
dreams of Polyxena, daughter I love best.   80
In my dreams I learned fear.

O gods below earth, keep safe my son,
the only anchor left to my house.
Hidden in snowbound Thrace, he lives
guarded by his father's friend.

Something new comes,
new bursts of grief in our grieving.
Never before has my heart so relentlessly
pounded, shuddered.

The soul of Helenus my prophet-son,   90
my daughter Cassandra—
women of Troy, where shall I find them?
They could read the truth in these dreams.

For I saw a fawn,
saw that a wolf's bloody teeth were slashing her bared
                                                     throat,
saw that necessity tore her away from my lap.
And I fear still more.
Achilles' ghost—
I saw it stride the earth heaped on the tomb
and it claimed as a last prize   100
one of us, a Trojan woman.
Not her, oh not her!
                    Divine might of heaven,
push this away from my own child, I beg you.

> *The* CHORUS *of captive women enters from the side*
> *tents and moves into the orchestra.* HECUBA *stands and*
> *listens with dignity.*

CHORUS (*chanting severally*) —Hecuba, here, I am coming.

—Coming in haste from my master's tent.

—The tent assigned to me by lot
   when I was taken slave.

—A slave driven out of my city, Troy,
   spear-hunted, trapped by the Greeks.   110

—I cannot lift the weight you bear.

—I come laden with heavy news.

—My lady, I come to herald pain.

—The Greeks met in full assembly. Word comes

they decreed a sacrifice. Achilles
claims your child.

                    —He strode on his tomb.
He appeared, as you know, armored in gold
and held back the ships when they put to sea,
canvas already straining at the stays.   120

—He shouted, he howled,
"Where, Greeks, where would you sail
leaving my tomb without its last prize?"

—And a wave of discord broke.
Argument divided that spear-proud host,
some eager to give the tomb its sacrifice,
others roaring NO!

—Agamemnon pressed for your good
because the one who is quick with prophecy
sleeps in his bed.   130

                    —But Theseus' two sons,
branches of Athens' tree, spoke with two voices
to state their one thought,
and they agreed that Achilles' tomb
be crowned with new-blossomed blood.

—"Cassandra's bed
or the spear of Achilles—
which would *you* put first?"

—And the rush of words, yes and no,
was balanced until   140
that shifty-hearted butcher knife,
that sweet-coaxing, pandering
son of Laertes persuades the army
not to reject the best of all Greeks
for the life of a slave, a sacrifice.

—Otherwise one of the dead,
    standing before Persephone, could say
    Greeks are ungrateful to Greeks
    who fell on Troy's plains
    and died for their country.   150

—And Odysseus will come, he will
    drag your foal away from your breast,
    out of your old arms.

                        —He wastes no time.

—Go to the temples.

                    —Go to the altars.
—Kneel before Agamemnon. Beg him.

—Cry out, beg the gods—gods in heaven,
    gods below earth.

—Prayer will save you from being made childless.   160
    or else you must see her thrown on that tomb.

—A virgin stained red.

—Blood on her gold-clad neck.

—Blood in a gleaming black gush.

HECUBA (*chanting*)
    No!
    What can misery cry out?
    What prayer, what pain, what dirge?
    Made more helpless in my old and helpless years,
    caught in slavery I cannot bend to,
    cannot bear—oh no!   170

    Who comes to help me? What kin,

what country? My husband, gone.
Gone, gone my sons.
This path, that path, which
shall I take? Where shall I go? Where find
a god, a force, a defender?

(*to the* CHORUS)

Woemongers, women of Troy,
you mongers of cruel woe,
you destroy, you destroy me.
 My life no longer holds   180
 a light I want to see.

Feet, be willing to carry me,
carry these old bones
back to the tent.

   Daughter, my daughter,
come, come out, listen to your mother,
your most unlucky mother.

    POLYXENA *enters from* AGAMEMNON'S *tent.*

O child—you should know—I hear such,
such rumors spread about your life.

POLYXENA (*chanting throughout this passage in response to*
   HECUBA'S *chant*)
   Mother, mother, why shout? What news?   190
   You flush me from cover
   like a frightened bird.

HECUBA Grieve, grieve with me, child.

POLYXENA Why grieve? This prelude scares me.

HECUBA Grieve, grieve for your life.

POLYXENA Speak. Stop hiding your secret.
          I'm shivering, shivering, mother.
          Why do you moan?

HECUBA   O child, child of a luckless mother.

POLYXENA What would you tell me?   200

HECUBA   Sacrifice. Yours. On Achilles' tomb.
          The Greeks, all the Greeks
          require it be done.

POLYXENA Mother, poor mother, how can your tongue
          be so cruel? Mother, tell me,
          tell *me* what you know.

HECUBA   I hear, child, a desperate rumor.
          The message comes that the Greeks have voted
          your life away.

POLYXENA How dreadfully your pain brims over!   210
          O mother, your years have brought you no joy.
          Once more an outrage
          hateful past words
          strikes down from heaven to hurt you.

          No more will your child
          be helpless with you in your helpless age,
          no more share slavery.

          Helpless, you must watch
          your helpless young, your calf,
          dragged from your arms,   220
          throat cut and consigned
          to Hades' dark earth
              where I shall lie
              sorrowing among the dead.

          I weep for you, grieving mother.

34

For you, my tears, my dirges.
My life will be seized and slashed open.
I cannot lament it, no.
                    To die
is my chance for happiness.   230

CHORUSLEADER (*speaking*) Look. Odysseus comes, stepping briskly.
              Hecuba, he'll give you news firsthand.

                    ODYSSEUS *enters left with an escort of Greek soldiers.*
                    POLYXENA *steps back and listens quietly to the following*
                                                              exchange.

ODYSSEUS Madam, I think you know of the vote cast
          and the army's decision. I bring you formal word.
          The Greeks have decreed that your daughter Polyxena
          be sacrificed before the earthmound of Achilles' grave.
          They choose me to take and escort
          the girl. And when the offering is made,
          a priest will officiate—Achilles' son.
          Do you know *your* duty?   240
          Not to let yourself be torn from her by force,
          not to contest my warrant with your fists,
          but bow to the strength of your troubles.
          Even in bad times, it's prudent
              to use common sense.

HECUBA Why, why
        must I face a struggle?
        Why must I moan and weep?
        Torn from my home, I did not die—
            I should have died!   250
        But God did not destroy me. He saves my life
        that I may suffer even greater loss.

                                          (*to* ODYSSEUS)

        But if a slave may ask a free man

questions not meant to offend or sting the heart,
then you must give answers,
and I who ask will listen.

ODYSSEUS Go ahead. I don't begrudge you the time.

HECUBA Remember when you came to Troy, a spy
wearing shapeless rags? Your eyes bled
the fear of death, the tears clotted in your beard.   260

ODYSSEUS I remember, I didn't take it lightly.

HECUBA But Helen knew you and told only me?

ODYSSEUS I recall coming into great danger.

HECUBA You humbled yourself, embracing my knees?

ODYSSEUS Yes, like a condemned man, my hand on your robes.

HECUBA So I saved you? I sent you out of my country?

ODYSSEUS Yes, and today I still see the sun.

HECUBA What did you say *then* when you were *my* slave?

ODYSSEUS I found a rush of words to keep me from dying.

HECUBA Do you smell the stench in your designs?   270
You admit that I treated you well.
But are you fair to me? No!
You use your power to cause me pain.
You people who grew up ignorant of gratitude,
who lust for acclaim bought by crowd-coaxing tongues—
I do not want to know a single one of you
who think nothing of abusing friends
so long as your smooth speeches lull the mob.

What chicanery tricked the Greeks
into voting slaughter of this child?   280
Do they feel bound to make human sacrifice

on that tomb where they should kill a steer?
Or if Achilles wants a death to pay for his death,
what justice that he target her for slaughter?
She never injured him—not once!

Helen—he must claim *her* blood to soak his tomb.
She killed him. She led him to Troy.
And if the captive picked for death must be
the one most beautiful, we are exempt.
Helen's face and form command all eyes,   290
and Helen's acts are not less wrong than ours.

Justice—I appeal first for justice.
And more: the debt you owe me now comes due.
Bear with me. You admit clinging to my hand,
touching this old cheek, kneeling to beg my mercy.

> HECUBA *kneels in suppliance, touching* ODYSSEUS'
> *knees. As she mentions the ritual gestures of supplica-*
> *tion, she performs them.*

My turn now. I cling, I touch, I call in
your debt of gratitude, I beg your mercy.
Do not tear my child from my arms.
Do not kill her. Enough of my children have died.
In her I remember joy and forget great loss.   300
She is my better self, my consolation,
my country, nurse, staff, guide.

The strong should not abuse their strength,
nor the fortunate think Chance will bless them forever.
I know. Once I was blessed. Not now.
One single day saw all I lived for lost.

> HECUBA *again touches* ODYSSEUS' *bearded cheek in*
> *supplication.*

But, O my friend, show me respect,
take pity. Go to the Greek army.
Warn that there will be just cause for anger

if you now kill women whom you did not kill   310
when first you tore them from their altars.
          Then you took pity.
And your laws forbid equally
spilling the blood of free man *and* slave.
Your prestige counts. No matter how you speak,
you will persuade them. High repute and low
may speak the same words but not with the same force.

CHORUS No human heart is set so hard
          that hearing the grave music of your dirge,
          your keening, would not bring tears.   320

          ODYSSEUS *pulls* HECUBA *to her feet and moves away*
                                              from her.

ODYSSEUS Hecuba, be instructed.
                Do not let your imagination
          find an enemy in one who gives you sound advice.
          I stand ready to save your person because chance
          let it save mine. I can say nothing more
          nor retract one thing that has been said.
          Troy is taken. The army's chief made his demand.
          For him your daughter will be sacrificed.
          Most countries show weakness—you know this—
          when the man truly noble and brave   330
          fails to be rewarded more than baser men.
          We think, woman, that Achilles deserves full honors.
          He died, our finest man, for Greece.
          Regard him alive as a friend, disregard him
          now he's dead—would that not shame us?

          So much for that. But what will people say
          if troops muster again and war comes?
          Will we choose to fight or to put our own lives first
          in a world where our dead lie dishonored?
          As for me, each day that I live may bring   340
          next to nothing. Yet, I have everything my life needs.

But I want my tomb thought worthy of tribute.
Such recognition endures.

But if you say, Pity me, I suffer,
I answer, Some of us are not less sorrow-struck—
grey-haired women, old men, brides, too,
deprived of their highborn young husbands
whose corpses rot covered by Troy's dust.

Accept your lot.
And we—if we do wrong to honor courage,   350
then we stand convicted of our ignorance.
But you foreigners do not treat friends as friends
nor pay respect to those who died
in a moral cause.
   Thus, Greece is fortune-blessed
while you barbarians receive
exactly what your notions call for.

CHORUS (*wailing*) The slave's lot—to know pure evil without cease,
  to bear what no one ought, to be crushed by force!

HECUBA Daughter, oh my words about your killing,   360
  put vainly in the air, disappear.

         POLYXENA *comes forward.*

But you—if you have more strength than your mother,
be quick, become a nightingale singing notes
so clear they stop this theft of life.
Stir pity. Grasp Odysseus' knees. Persuade.
You can change his mind, for he has children, too.
Make him pity the chance that strikes a child.

POLYXENA I see, Odysseus, that your right hand
  hides inside your cloak and your face turns aside
  so that I cannot touch your bearded cheek.   370
  At ease! You have escaped the Zeus

who guards all suppliants.
Yes, I will go. Necessity is kind,
for I *wish* to die. If not, I'd seem
a woman broken but rejecting death.

Why should I live? My earliest memory:
my father lord over all Trojans.
And I grew, cherished, reared with bright hope
for a king's bride. Not small the rivalry
about whose court, whose fire would give me welcome.   380
And I, degraded now, was princess
among Trojan women, most admired of her virgins,
a goddess except in one way—I must die.

But now I am slave. That name alone,
harsh name, makes me lust for death.
I might chance, too, on a brutal master
who'd haggle and trade silver coins for me—
sister to Hector and the many others,
and he'd constrain me to his needs—grind corn, make
                                                 bread,
sweep dirt from his house, stand at the loom,   390
each day know grief. He'll force constraint on me.
And a slave, bought who knows where, will foul
my bed that was reserved for kings.
No! I forfeit my view of this sunlight—
free—as I hand my body to the god of death.

Lead me, Odysseus. Let this contest for me stop.
For I can see no hope, no grounds to think
that glory might again invest our days.
And you, mother, try not to stop us
with speeches or tugging hands. But agree that I should   400
die before my dignity is made ugly by shame.
One not accustomed to the taste of cruelty
endures it but bends her neck to the yoke of anguish.
Dying would be better luck than living,
for life without moral beauty inflicts endless pain.

CHORUS   Nobility—how deep and terrible its stamp
on those wellborn. And when actions enhance
a good name, it wins still greater dignity.

HECUBA   Beautiful words, my daughter, but in their beauty
my grief lies waiting.   410

(*to* ODYSSEUS)

Odysseus, if you need
to show Achilles gratitude, yet cast
no blame on Greeks, do not kill her.
Take me instead. Lead me to his grave.
Kill me without a qualm. *I* gave birth to Paris
whose arrows shot down Achilles.

ODYSSEUS   Old woman, Achilles' ghost did not
demand your throat be cut but hers.

HECUBA   Then kill me with my daughter.
Earth and that corpse who makes demands   420
shall drink twice as much blood.

ODYSSEUS   One death—your girl's—is enough. No more.
I wish we did not gain from even one.

HECUBA   I am constrained to die with my child.

ODYSSEUS   Who gives orders here? My master?

HECUBA   Ivy to oak—that's how I'll cling to her.

ODYSSEUS   No. Listen to someone with better sense.

HECUBA   I will not let go of my child.

ODYSSEUS   I will not depart and leave her here.

POLYXENA Mother, listen to me. And you, son of Laertes,   430
          unbend toward a parent with good cause for distress.
          And you, poor mother, don't fight power.
          Do you want to be thrown down, agèd flesh bleeding,
          and want to be shoved away, manhandled,
          hauled off in disgrace by some callow soldier?
          No, not you! That does not befit you.

          But, mother I love, give me your sweet hand,
          let me press my cheek to yours.
          Never again, but now for the last time I shall
          see the rays, the bright circle of the sun.   440
          Accept my last greeting, my last goodbye.
          My mother who gave me birth, I go to my dying.

                    POLYXENA *and* HECUBA *embrace.*

HECUBA While I, daughter, live on as a slave.

POLYXENA No bridegroom, no wedding songs for me.

HECUBA You, child, win pity. My lot is anguish.

POLYXENA I'll lie in Hades separated from you.

HECUBA No! What shall I do? Where will my life end?

POLYXENA Freedom was my birthright, but I die a slave.

HECUBA And I have lost all my fifty children.

POLYXENA What do I say to Hector and your husband?   450

HECUBA That I am the most anguished of women.

POLYXENA O breasts that sweetly nursed me.

HECUBA O daughter, your luck—spoilt before it ripened.

POLYXENA Farewell, mother. Give Cassandra my farewell—

HECUBA Others fare well. Your mother cannot.

POLYXENA —and my brother Polydorus here in Thrace.

HECUBA Does he live? I doubt it. I have no luck.

POLYXENA He *is* alive. He'll close *your* eyes when you die.

HECUBA I *have* died. Cruelty kills me before my time.

POLYXENA Take your prize, Odysseus. Cover my face.   460
Wails, dirges—before my dying I have made
my mother's heart dissolve in tears, I melt in her tears.
O light! I may still speak your name
and claim my brief share in you as I
walk to the sword and Achilles' grave.

> As POLYXENA *speaks,* ODYSSEUS *slowly veils her head*
> *with a corner of her robe.* ODYSSEUS, POLYXENA, *and*
> *the soldiers exit left, in that order. The soldiers follow at*
> *a respectful distance and do not touch* POLYXENA.

HECUBA O God, no!
My head reels. My legs won't hold me.
Child! Touch me, stretch out your hand, give it.
Don't leave me childless.

(*to the* CHORUS)

Friends, I am destroyed.   470

(*sinking to the ground*)

And so would I see Spartan Helen.
Her eyes flashed, her lovely lustful eyes, and she shamed,
she burnt Troy's blessedness.

HECUBA, *supine, shrouds herself with her robes and lies
on the ground with corpselike stillness.*

CHORUS (*singing and dancing*) Seawind, sail-filling wind,
who makes the swift ships
leap through onrolling waves,

where will you carry my sorrow?
Shall I go to a house
as a piece of bought goods, as a slave?
Or go to a Dorian harbor?   480

Shall I go to Phthia?
There, so they tell me, the purest of rivers
fathers the crops in glistening green fields.

Oars, sea-sweeping oars,
will you bring my sad life
home to an island?

The isle where the first palm and laurel
sprouted, honoring Leto
with gifts: holy shade and trunks to grip
as she labored to bear Zeus twin children?   490

There with the virgins of Delos
shall I sing praising goddess Artemis,
praise to her arrows and gold crown?

Shall I go to the city of Pallas?
And there on Athena's saffron robe
shall I harness

the foals to her gleaming chariot
with intricate stitches
of flower-steeped threads?
Or shall I weave Titans   500

as Zeus blazed his double lightning
    and seared them with death?

Oh how I grieve for my children.
I grieve for my fathers' earth, for my home.
    And I still see

the smoke and the burning and Greek
    spears. And I am called slave
    in a land of exile,
    made to leave Asia,

made to become Europe's servant   510
    and bride to my death.

                                    TALTHYBIUS *enters left.*

TALTHYBIUS Where might I find Troy's onetime queen?
            Trojan women, where is Hecuba?

CHORUSLEADER Near you, Talthybius—there, on her back,
              shut away inside her robes.

TALTHYBIUS My god! Zeus, *do* you watch over human lives?
            Or do we cling to such belief in vain,
            [falsely sure that more-than-human powers exist,]
            when Chance, blind Chance, rules us till we die?
            Was she not queen of the gold-proud Trojans,   520
            nor wife to Priam glad in his great wealth?
            And now spears have torn her city from its roots,
            and she—a slave, old, childless—lies there,
            common dust crowning her head.
            I too, I too am old, but I would rather
            die than let chance plunge me
                in the ugliness of shame.

                                    (*to* HECUBA)

Stand. Lift yourself.
Lift up that white, white head.

HECUBA   Away, whoever you are, away.   530
           Let my body rest. Why intrude on grief?

                    HECUBA *begins to rise slowly.*

TALTHYBIUS   I am Talthybius, my lady, servant to the Greeks.
           Agamemnon sent me for you.

HECUBA   A friend, come to take me also to that tomb
           for sacrifice—is that what the Greeks decide?
           Oh yes! Hurry, hurry, help me, old man.

TALTHYBIUS   Your dead child, my lady—you are to bury her.
           That's why I come, so ordered
           by Atreus's two sons and all the Greeks.

HECUBA   God, no! I am not to die? You come   540
           only to bring cutting words?
                      O young one,
           you *are* gone, torn from your mother
           who learns once more the pain of losing a child.

           And how did you end her life? With due respect?
           Or as an enemy, in ways too
               terrible to mention?
           Old man, tell the truth, though it gives no comfort.

TALTHYBIUS   My lady, you ask me to reap my tears twice.
           My eyes filled when I watched your child die.   550
           Now memory must see her die again.

           They were all there—the Greek army in full strength,
           there by the tomb for your girl's sacrifice.
           And Achilles' son took Polyxena's hand
           and placed her on top of the grave-mound.

I stood nearby.
And young soldiers, specially chosen, followed,
hands ready to keep your calf from bolting.
And the son of Achilles takes in his two hands
a brimming goblet, pure gold, and raises   560
libations to his dead father. And he signals me
to call the whole army to silence.

I took my station and called out the order:
"Silence, Greeks. All keep silence.
Keep still. Silence." And not a ripple swept the crowd.
And he spoke: "O son of Peleus, my father,
receive this wine that summons up and calms
the dead. And come, taste a darker drink,
a girl's unwatered blood, the army's gift and mine.
And turn your dead eyes peacefully on us at last   570
and let the hulls go, let the hawsers loose,
and let the ships sail from Troy in peace,
grant us all a safe return home."

So he spoke,
        and the whole army echoed, "Safe return home."
Then, taking his sword by the gold-covered hilt,
he unsheathed it and gave a quick nod
to the chosen young men: Take the virgin.
But she saw him and gave her own clear orders:
"Listen, Greeks who laid my city waste,   580
I volunteer my death. Let no hand touch me,
for I am glad to offer you my throat.
Set me free so, by the gods, I die free
when you do your killing. Born a queen, I
would feel shame to be called slave among the dead.

A wave of approval broke, and Lord Agamemnon
told the young guards to let go of the virgin.
And they, the instant they heard that order
come from the chief in command, let her go.
And when she heard authority's words,   590

she grasped her robe and tore it wide open
from shoulder straight down to her navel
and showed breasts that gleamed like a statue's
carved to honor the gods, and she knelt on one knee
to say the most courageous last words:
"Look, young soldier. If you would strike
my breast, strike here. But if my throat
is what you want, my neck is bared—here."

And he, unwilling yet willing in his pity,
cuts her windpipe with the iron sword.   600
Springs gushed forth. But she even in her dying
took great care to fall modestly, hiding
all that should be hidden from men's eyes.

Then, when sacrifice had stopped her breathing,
none of the Greeks performed the same labor,
but some strewed green leaves over her body,
while some brought pine logs to build her
a pyre. And the man who brought nothing
heard the bringers accuse him: "How can you
stand there, you no-good, hands empty,   610
no robe, no gift for the young one?
Nothing—is that what you give to the bravest,
the brightest in soul?"
                              Hecuba, your child
is dead. Of all the world's women, I see you
as luckiest in your child and most ill-used by Chance.

CHORUS What does it mean—that misery boiled over, scalding
Priam's house and people? How fierce, the gods' constraints!

HECUBA Daughter,
              what single grief shall I look at? I don't know.   620
Many, many press close. And if I seize this one,
that one does not let me go, and out of it
another heartache summons me, grief crowds on grief.
And now, your suffering—I cannot

wash it from my thoughts, cannot help wailing.
But you keep me from excessive tears by your
inborn grace.

What does it mean—that poor soil
given its chance by the gods, bears abundant grain,
but fertile soil, deprived of what it needs, will yield   630
a poor crop? How different people are!
The worthless person stays forever base
while the man of nobility *is* noble,
and no disaster drives him to deplete
that inborn nature—he is good forever.
Do parents count for more, or education?
Parents, to be sure! Yet a moral education
will teach nobility. And a person well taught comes
to understand shame's ugliness
        by learning what is beautiful.   640

Oh how my mind shoots its arrows—to what use?

(*to* TALTHYBIUS)

You, go, make it clear to the Greeks
that no one touch my child, that the mob
keep off. When thousands bear arms, well you know
the mob's unchecked, the sailors run more lawless
than wildfire, and one who does no wrong *is* wrong.

TALTHYBIUS *exits left.*

(*to the* SERVING WOMAN)

And you, take a pail, old servant.
Dip it in the sea, and bring me saltwater.
For the last time I'd bathe my child—
bride and ghost's bride, virgin and virgin's ghost—   650
wash her and bury her as she deserves. But how?
I cannot, I have—why this confusion?

Small ornaments, at least—I'll collect them
from the captive women in these tents, if
anyone, escaping her new master's notice, still keeps
some fine thing smuggled from her own home.

> The SERVING WOMAN *exits left.*

O walls and roofs of home, Chance smiled on your halls.
O Priam, you owned wealth and beauty, you fathered
strong sons, and I, gone grey, was their mother.
How we all come to nothing, stripped of the spirit   660
once ours. How people preen and puff themselves,
one because the world's goods overflow his house,
another because the citizens flatter him.
All nothing, nothing but wishful thinking
and idle talk. The richest among us
is he who chances on no evil day by day.

> HECUBA *exits into* AGAMEMNON'S *tent.*

CHORUS (*singing and dancing*) My fate gave me to disaster,
my fate gave me over to sorrow

the moment the pines on Mt. Ida
were cut down by Paris   670

to build the ship he would steer through high waves
to the bed of Helen
     most beautiful woman on whom
the gold-shining Sun casts light.

My grief and a force far stronger—
constraint—come circling around me.

Out of one man's mad folly,
for all who lived by Troy's river

ruin burst forth, seaborne disaster swept in,
and discord flows rapid   680

when Paris, a herdsman on Ida,
judges three daughters of gods.

The outcome, spears and murder
    and my home dishonored.
And laments also rise
    by the banks of a sunlit Greek river
where a Spartan girl cries alone in her room

and a mother mourning dead children
lifts hands to her head
and tears out grey hair   690
    and rakes down her cheeks
with nails gone
    bloody from her sacrifice.

The SERVING WOMAN *enters left with attendants bearing*
                                            a covered corpse.

SERVING WOMAN (*loudly*) Women, where is Hecuba? Poor thing,
she wins at grief. Over every man and woman
she wins. No one will dispute her crown.

CHORUSLEADER What is your foul tongue shouting?
Your hurtful cries don't pause for rest.

SERVING WOMAN (*indicating the corpse*) I bring Hecuba this pain. In ugly
                                                          times
it's not easy to put pretty words in my mouth.   700

CHORUSLEADER And here she comes.
Give her your words.

                        HECUBA *enters from the tent.*

SERVING WOMAN Oh my lady, I can't find words for your torment.
You're destroyed, no light left to see,
no child, no husband, no homeland. You're ruined.

HECUBA You say nothing new. You taunt me.
But why come bearing Polyxena's
body? We've heard the Greeks have
busied all hands for her funeral.

SERVING WOMAN (*aside*) She does *not* know. She mourns Polyxena.   710
There's new pain that she has not grasped.

HECUBA Torment! Not the one who sings out
prophecy, oh not my Cassandra?

SERVING WOMAN She's alive. You wail her name but make no sound
for this one.

> *The* SERVING WOMAN *uncovers the corpse.*

Look at the body I've covered.
It's a shock to see hope gone all wrong.

HECUBA (*moans*)
My son, he's dead—Polydorus,
kept safe in the Thracian's house.
A final wound. I breathe but I do not live.   720

(*chanting*)

Child, my child,
I'll raise you a song, the measure
that vengeance enacts. Made wild,
I learn new strains of grief.

SERVING WOMAN (*speaking*) Then you know what happened to your son?

HECUBA (*chanting*)
Past all belief, the shocking shocking sight.
Volley on volley, grief crowds on grief.
Never again shall my days break
free of groans, free of tears.

CHORUSLEADER What does it mean—   730
                    these blows
                            that keep striking?

    HECUBA (*chanting*)
                Child, O my child,
                what destiny kills you, what doom makes you lie here,
                what human hand?

SERVING WOMAN (*speaking*) I don't know. I found him on the shore.

    HECUBA (*chanting*)
                Drowned and cast up on the smooth sand?
                Cut down by a bloody spear?

SERVING WOMAN (*speaking*) The surf washed him ashore.

    HECUBA (*chanting*)
                Now, oh now I'm taught the meaning   740
                sent in last night's dream. No fancy,
                that shadow spreading its black wings.
                I saw you, it was you, child,
                no longer living in Zeus' radiant light.

CHORUSLEADER Who killed him?
                    Did you read
                            that in your dream?

    HECUBA (*chanting*)
                My friend, my friend, the Thracian commander
                with whom his old father placed him for hiding.

CHORUSLEADER What do you imply?   750
                    He killed
                            for the gold?

    HECUBA (*chanting*)
                No words for this, no name, it more than stuns,

not godly, not bearable—where *are* friendship's laws?
Damn you! Oh how you hacked my son's flesh,
your steel blade cutting his arms, his legs,
and you showed him no pity.

CHORUSLEADER Woman who has
                    known more pain
                            than any other living soul,   760
              heaven insists
                    that you bear
                            whatever burdens you most.

              But the master comes—Agamemnon.
              Silence, friends, be silent.

                              AGAMEMNON *and his escort enter left.*

AGAMEMNON Hecuba, why so slow to bury your child?
              Talthybius gave us your message—
              no Greek to lay a finger on the girl.
              We've gone along with that; we do not touch her.
              But you amaze me by dawdling here.   770
              I've come to fetch you. Where she is, all's been managed
              beautifully—if such things can be beautiful.

                              (*seeing the body of* POLYDORUS)

              Hah! Who's this—the man beside the tent?
              Dead, Trojan, certainly not Greek—
              his clothing tells me that.

HECUBA (*aside*)
              You wretched woman—I speak to you and mean
              myself. What to do? Embrace Agamemnon's knees,
              beg his help? Or bear my torment in silence?

AGAMEMNON Why hide your face and turn your back?
              Why wail but tell me nothing? Who is this?   780

HECUBA *(aside)*
　　But if he should think me slave and enemy
　　and shove me off, my pain would grow.

AGAMEMNON You know I was not born a prophet.
　　I hear you but cannot follow your thoughts.

HECUBA *(aside)*
　　Or do I miscalculate—seeing him
　　as hostile when he means no ill?

AGAMEMNON All right, if you don't want to speak, we've reached
　　the same point. For I don't want to hear.

HECUBA *(aside)*
　　Without this man I cannot avenge my children.
　　Why think further? Necessity gives me   790
　　courage to act. Succeed or fail, I'll take that chance.

　　　　　HECUBA *goes to* AGAMEMNON, *kneels, and makes the*
　　　　　　　　　　　　　　　　gestures of supplication.

　　Agamemnon, I touch your knees, your bearded cheek,
　　your god-guided right hand. I beg your help.

AGAMEMNON What do you crave? Freedom?
　　That's easy.

HECUBA No, no! Revenge on criminals,
　　and I'll be slave for all my days to come.

AGAMEMNON But why call for *our* help?

HECUBA Not for reasons you can imagine, my lord.
　　You do see this body and the tears I shed?   800

AGAMEMNON Of course. But I can't see what comes next.

HECUBA I gave him birth. I carried him in my womb.

AGAMEMNON Which child, then, is *this* one?

HECUBA *Not* one of those sons who died beneath Troy's walls.

AGAMEMNON Are you saying you had still another?

HECUBA And not to my comforting, the one you see.

AGAMEMNON But where was he when your country was destroyed?

HECUBA His father sent him away so he would not die.

AGAMEMNON Where did he go, this one you singled out?

HECUBA To this country where we found him dead.   810

AGAMEMNON To the ruler of this land? Polymestor?

HECUBA Yes, sent here to guard the most bitter gold.

AGAMEMNON How did it happen? Who killed him?

HECUBA Who indeed but the Thracian, our friend.

AGAMEMNON Did he lust that eagerly for gold?

HECUBA Oh yes, as soon as he knew of Troy's fall.

AGAMEMNON Where did you find him? Did someone bring his body?

HECUBA This woman. She found him on the shore.

AGAMEMNON Looking for him? Or busy at something else?

HECUBA She went to bring seawater to bathe Polyxena.   820

AGAMEMNON So his host killed him and cast the body out.

HECUBA Yes, and the waves tossed his knife-shredded flesh.

AGAMEMNON You've suffered more than anyone can measure.

HECUBA I am destroyed. No further suffering is left.

AGAMEMNON Could any woman be less fortunate?

HECUBA None, except Misfortune herself.

But now, the reason that I grasp your knees—
please hear me.
                    And if you think the gods approve my
                                                    suffering,
I'll accept that. But if you think otherwise,   830
avenge me on that man, that most ungodly friend.
Fearing neither those below nor those on high,
he has done the most ungodly crime.
A man who often shared my food, a man I counted
first among my friends, to whom I gave
every courtesy—he did premeditated
murder. Yet, the murder planned, he gave no thought
to decent burial but made the sea his rubbish pit.

True, I am a slave without strength. But the gods
are strong and so is that which forms their power—   840
the law of custom. For, this age-old law
      confirms our faith in gods
and gives us lives that can distinguish right from wrong.
Keeping the law depends on you.
          If it's transgressed,
and if no punishment is dealt to those who murder
friends or plunder the gods' holy places,
then no justice—none—exists for humankind.

Let your sense of shame give you compassion.
Have pity. Like a painter, stand back,   850
look at me and see my sorrows whole.
Once a queen, but now I am your slave,
once blessed with sons, now old, without my sons,
without a home, alone, struggling to the utmost,
helpless—

57

AGAMEMNON *tries to pull away.*

No! Where are you going?
I'll accomplish nothing. Oh helpless.
Why do we spend our short lives straining,
craving after knowledge of all sorts but one—
Persuasion, who alone is mankind's queen?   860
Why no zeal in us to hire a teacher
and learn the art so perfectly
that we persuade and we obtain?

Without that art, how may anyone hope
        to come out well?
Those who were my sons are mine no more,
and I, a captive ugly in my shame, am lost.
I see the smoke still rolling up from Troy.

Perhaps it is pointless for me to put forward
Love's divine name. But I shall do it.   870
Pressed against your ribs, my daughter sleeps,
my child possessed by prophecy, Cassandra.
How, my lord, will you acknowledge love's delights?
Or for the loveliest embraces in your bed,
what thanks, what fee will my child gain,
        and I for her?
For out of darkness, out of night's enchantments comes
the strongest drive toward thanks that flesh can know.
Listen to me. Do you see that dead boy?
Do him honor, and you honor kin, your bedmate's   880
brother.

        One thought still looks for words.
If only Daedalus could work his wonders,
or some god, to give my arms a voice,
my hands a voice, and my hair and feet,
then all would clasp your knees in concert
crying out my plea in all possible ways.

My master, most shining light among the Greeks,
be moved. Lend your hand to an old woman, a hand

for vengeance, though it come to nothing. Be fair.   890
For the man born noble and good always serves justice
and finds fit consequences for a crime.

AGAMEMNON *extends a hand and lifts* HECUBA *from her*
suppliant posture.

CHORUS What does it mean?
          Everything crashes together on mortal flesh.
The world's constraint, not bound by human laws,
can turn our fiercest enemies to friends
and stir up hate in those who once meant well.

AGAMEMNON I do have pity, Hecuba, for you,
          your son, your misfortune, your suppliant hands.
And I want for the gods' sake, the sake of justice   900
to help somehow
          to give you justice on that godless friend.
But if things work out for you, the army
must not take the notion that I
plot the murder of Thrace's king
          as thanks to Cassandra.
Uneasiness sweeps down on me.
The army thinks that man its ally,
the dead one its enemy. And if he's dear to you,
that's your concern, not shared by the army.   910
See it my way. I'm willing, yes,
to work with you, eager to give you aid,
but slow to let the Greeks assign me any blame.

HECUBA I see.
I see that no one alive, no one, is free.
For some are slaves to money, others to chance
or majority rule or man-made laws
that keep them from acting on their own good sense.
You're frightened, you bend to the crowd's beliefs.
I shall set you free, free from that fear.   920
Be my accomplice,
          should I plan harm to him who killed my son,

only in the knowing, not the doing.
But if the Greeks should give outcry or start to help
the Thracian when he enjoys what he deserves,
hold them off. Don't seem to act for me.
The rest? Be confident. I shall manage it—beautifully.

AGAMEMNON How? What will you do? Snatch up a sword
in your old hand and kill that barbarian?
Give him poison? And who will help?   930
Is there a helping hand? Where will you find friends?

HECUBA The tents hide a mass of Trojans.

AGAMEMNON You mean the captives, the Greeks' plunder?

HECUBA With them I'll take my vengeance on the murderer.

AGAMEMNON Just how can women overpower men?

HECUBA Sheer numbers. Add our wiles, and we're invincible.

AGAMEMNON Invincible? Womankind deserves contempt.

HECUBA What! Did not women kill Aegyptus' sons
and empty Lemnos of every last male?
Enough! I put aside such argument.   940

(*indicating the* SERVING WOMAN)

Give safe conduct through the army's lines to this
woman.

(*to the* SERVING WOMAN)

And you, go to our Thracian friend.
Say this: "Hecuba, once queen of Troy, summons you
in your own interest no less than hers. And bring
your sons. They, too, must be acquainted with her
information."

The SERVING WOMAN *exits right with an*
escort provided by AGAMEMNON.

(*to* AGAMEMNON)

And the girl just sacrificed—
you, Agamemnon, delay Polyxena's funeral.
Let brother and sister, a mother's twofold grief,   950
be burnt in one flame and buried in one grave.

Attendants of HECUBA *exit left with the body of*
POLYDORUS.

AGAMEMNON As you wish. And you know, if the army should
set sail, I would not grant this favor.
But as it is, the gods send no fair wind.
The sails lie slack. We are constrained to wait.
May you somehow succeed. It's everyone's concern,
public and private, to see the evildoer
fall on evil times while the upright prosper.

AGAMEMNON *exits left with his escort.*

CHORUS (*singing and dancing*) You, O my homeland Troy,
will be named no more among unplundered cities.   960
The Greek cloud surrounding you hides
the waste made by spears, driving spears.

And you have been shorn of crowning towers
and you have been stained—
my heart grieves—by smoke-blackened flames.
City brought low,
        no more shall I set foot within you.

Death came to me at midnight,
the evening meal over, eyes sweetly drowsy,
and when he had done with dancing the songs   970
and making burnt offerings to gods,

61

my husband lay in our bedroom,
his spear on its peg.
He never saw what the sea brought—
mobs of men shouting.
     O Troy, they have trampled upon you.

I was arranging my hair,
binding it up in ribbons for the night,
and a golden mirror's endless sunlight
held my gaze.   980
I would have laid me down upon the warm bed,

but up through the city rose
clamor, and this cry rang down through Troy:
O sons of Greeks, how soon, I ask how soon
you will lay the Trojan hill-fort waste
and sail for home?

Dear bed, leaving you I wore
tunic only, like a Spartan girl.
I clung heartsick to holy Artemis but
all in vain.   990
And I am swept, beholding my bedmate killed,

away on the salt sea, and as I
look back on my city, the ship
homeward bound moved its keel and severed me
forever from Troy's earth. I fainted then,
a woman brought low.

To the sister of God's two sons—Helen,
to Mt. Ida's shepherd, war-breeding Paris,
my gift, a curse!
Forcing me to leave my fathers' earth,   1000
they gave me death,

and I am cast out from my home by marriage
not marriage but some vengeful dirge.
May the salt sea never grant her passage.
May she never return to her fathers' home.

POLYMESTOR *and his sons enter right with their guards.*

POLYMESTOR My dearest friend Priam, O my dearest
Hecuba, I weep for you both and your city
and your daughter recently dead.

(sighs)

Nothing at all can be trusted, not good name,
not good luck. Moral actions turn out wrong.   1010
And it's the gods themselves make this jumble,
confusing us so we, not knowing what may happen,
will worship them. But why sing out
complaints? They give no help in outrunning sorrow.

But you, if you blame me at all for my absence,
hold back. I'm deep in the mountains when you
arrived in Thrace. But I'd just come home,
was just on the verge of going to see you,
when this servant of yours comes dashing at me
to give your message. I heard, and here I am.   1020

HECUBA I am ashamed to look you in the face,
Polymestor, while sorrows crowd and cover me.
You saw me first in my days of good fortune.
You see me now in altered circumstances—shamed,
nor can I look at you with steady eyes.
But do not think my manner expresses ill will,
Polymestor. No, for custom's law
binds women not to look men in the face.

POLYMESTOR Nothing strange in that. But what do you need?
Why did I come running here?   1030

HECUBA A private matter, one I wish
to discuss with you and your sons.
Order your guard to leave.

POLYMESTOR (*to the guards, who exit right*) Go.

(*to* HECUBA)

We are alone here and secure.
You are my friend, and the Greeks' armed forces
also bear me friendship. But make your need plain.
What must a man who prospers do for friends
who prosper not at all? I stand ready to help.

HECUBA Tell me first about the son who came   1040
from my hands and his father's to your house.
Polydorus—does he live?

POLYMESTOR Of course. In him your luck is good.

HECUBA Dearest friend, how well this news conveys your worth!

POLYMESTOR Now what would you like to know next?

HECUBA His mother—does he remember me?

POLYMESTOR Yes, and tried to visit you in secret.

HECUBA And the gold is safe? The gold he brought from Troy?

POLYMESTOR Safe, and closely guarded in my house.

HECUBA Keep it safe, and do not lust for your neighbor's goods. 1050

POLYMESTOR Never. My lady, I enjoy what's already mine.

HECUBA Can you guess what I want to tell you and your sons?

POLYMESTOR No, but your words will soon tell me.

HECUBA There exists—O longtime friend, how dear to me now—

POLYMESTOR What *is* it that I and my sons must know?

HECUBA —gold, the ancient buried treasure of Priam's house.

POLYMESTOR Do you want your son to know about it?

HECUBA Of course, and through you, a man who honors duty.

POLYMESTOR But why demand my children be here?

HECUBA Better, should you die, that they have the secret.   1060

POLYMESTOR Well said. You choose the wiser course.

HECUBA Do you know where Athena's temple stands in Troy?

POLYMESTOR The gold is there? What marks the spot?

HECUBA A black rock rising from the ground.

POLYMESTOR Anything more that you want to tell me?

HECUBA Save the heirlooms I smuggled from Troy.

POLYMESTOR Where are they? Hidden in your robes? Buried?

HECUBA Safe beneath the plunder heaped in the tents.

POLYMESTOR But where? This is the Greeks' naval encampment.

HECUBA The captive women have private quarters.   1070

POLYMESTOR Quarters I can trust? A place without men?

HECUBA No Greeks, no men—we women are alone.
But come into the tent—oh how the Greeks

chafe to sail home—come now.
When you've done all you must, you may leave
with your sons for the place where you housed my child.

> HECUBA, POLYMESTOR, *and his sons exit into the*
> *central tent.*

CHORUS (*singing*) You have not paid but you shall pay
          justice in full.
     Like someone falling
          overboard, no haven near,   1080
     you, too, shall fall away from heart's desire,
     your world a wreck. For the double debt
     owed Justice and the gods contains no clash.
     Ruin, ruin in committing wrong.
     Your high road of hope shall cheat you and lead you
     down to the god who owns death,
                              O man brought low,
     and a hand unacquainted with war
          shall cost you your life.

POLYMESTOR (*inside the tent*) My eyes, oh my eyes—I am blind!   1090

HALFCHORUS Did you hear the man's anguish, friends?

POLYMESTOR My children, my sons—you are murdered!

HALFCHORUS Friends, new wrongs have been done.

POLYMESTOR Run, run, but you won't get away.
          I'll batter these walls till they break.

> *Loud noises, as of a heavy missile striking the wall, are*
> *heard.*

CHORUS (*severally*)—Look! What blows come pelting from heavy hands!

—Should we rush in?

—Yes, now.

Hecuba needs our help.

HECUBA *enters with several women.*

HECUBA   Smash on, hold nothing back, keep pounding.   1100
Your eyes will never again see light
nor see alive the sons *I* killed.

CHORUSLEADER   My lady, you bested that—friend?
And truly did it just as you say?

HECUBA   You'll see for yourselves. He will come forth
blind, stumbling, groping his way on blind feet.
And you will see two bodies, the sons *I* killed
with help from Troy's noblest women. Justice
is mine.
                And see, he's coming now.   1110
I'll stand back, remove myself
from the rush of his anger,
            an anger he will never quell.

POLYMESTOR *stumbles from the tent and falls.*

POLYMESTOR   (*singing*) My eyes, oh eyes!
                Where run, where stand, where stop?
Four-footed, made a mountain animal,
I crawl, hands searching out the track.
This way, that—which way to turn,
to take these women, man-murdering women
who brought me down?   1120
                        Daughters of Troy,
            damn you, damn you.

Where do they flee, where go to ground?
Bleeding sockets, eyes made blind—if only you could
heal them, heal them, holy Sun,
and dazzle me with light.
Aaah, aaah,
hush! I hear the soft scurry

of women.
                    Where stalk that prey, where pounce   1130
to glut me on their flesh and bones,
to make a feast of such fierce animals?
Where go to sate me on ruin
that repays this outrage?
          Oh poor blind eyes!

But where *do* I go? Why leave my children
alone,
          sacrificed,
soon torn apart by death-crazed women
and thrown out on mountain rocks,   1140
          raw, bloody meat for dogs?
Where stand, where rest, where run?
Like a ship in port, sails furled,
I gather in my linen robe.
                    Where run
to guard my children in that deadly lair?

          POLYMESTOR'S *sons are carried from the tent by Trojan*
                  women and laid in the space occupied earlier by
                            POLYDORUS' *body.*

CHORUS Luckless man,
              how can you bear
                  the crimes worked against you?
        But, for your shameful,   1150
              ugly deeds,
                  the energy of heaven
        exacts
              this fearful price
                  that bends you low.

POLYMESTOR (*singing*) My eyes, oh my eyes!
          Yo! You Thracian spearmen, horsemen,
              all of you whose blood thrills to War!
          Yo! You Greeks, you sons of Atreus!

I shout, I howl, I who rule Thrace.   1160
Yo! In the gods' name, be quick, come!
Do you hear? Will you help? What now?
Women destroyed me,
women, women made captive in war.
What does it mean—this darkness I endure?

O ruined eyes, O life in ruin,
where find a foothold, where be driven?
Where will a wretch go?
     Fly, soaring up to the rooftree of sky
where hunter Orion and Dog Star at heel blaze   1170
     jets of fire straight from their eyes?
                        Or plunge
through the black-skinned water
     where Hades' ferryman bends his oars?

CHORUS We should forgive
     the man who suffers wrongs
          too great to bear
and would prefer
     self-made release
          from life.   1180

                 AGAMEMNON *and his escort enter left.*

AGAMEMNON What is this uproar? It holds no peace.
Echo made it ring and crash among the rocks
unsettling the army. And if we had not known
Troy's towers were long fallen to Greek spears,
this din would strike panic.

POLYMESTOR (*speaking*) Best friend! I know that voice. It's you,
Agamemnon. Do you see what is done to me?

AGAMEMNON I do.
Polymestor, who wants to destroy you?
Who blinded you and made your eyes weep blood?   1190

Who killed your sons? What bursting rage he had,
whoever he is, against you and your children.

POLYMESTOR Hecuba—she and those women war captives—
she destroyed me, no, more than destroyed me.

AGAMEMNON I am shocked!

(*to* HECUBA)

You did this as he claims?
Hecuba, *you* dared this boldness? Impossible.

POLYMESTOR She did!
You speak to her? She's near, somewhere near?
Turn me, tell me where she is. When I set   1200
hands on her, I'll tear her flesh to bloody scraps.

AGAMEMNON (*to* POLYMESTOR) What's wrong with you?

POLYMESTOR   By the gods, let me
catch her. My hands crave her flesh.

AGAMEMNON Stop! Don't be barbaric.
Argue your case. When I've heard your brief and hers,
I'll decide—justly—if you've earned your pain.

POLYMESTOR If it please you.
The youngest son of Hecuba and Priam
was Polydorus. His father Priam,   1210
who suspected that Troy would fall,
sent him out to me, to be reared in my house.
I killed him. And why did I kill him?
Listen: with clever foresight for your own good.
He was your enemy, that boy. Left alive,
he would regroup the Trojans and rebuild their home.
And the Greeks, knowing one of Priam's get lived,
would send their forces to make war again on Troy.

And going home, they'd trample Thrace's fields and take
the cattle. Troy's near neighbor would again reap   1220
Troy's defeat. My lord, Thrace is weary.

But Hecuba learned of her son's death,
and she entrapped me with a tale of something
Priam's family had hidden in Troy—
gold. And she takes me alone with my children
into the tent where no other man
        may see or overhear us.

I settle, relaxed, on a couch.
And many hands reach out from right and left
to welcome me, as with a friend, of course.   1230
Troy's daughters seat themselves.
        Some finger the Thracian weave
of my robes and hold the cloth to the sunlight,
and others, touching my Thracian spear in admiration,
strip me naked of robes and weapon both.
And the mothers among them, cooing praise,
play toss with my children, handing them on
till they are far, far from their father.
Then, out of a calm sea—can you imagine?—
knives spring sudden out of hiding in their robes.   1240
They stab my sons, while their companions seize me
like a prisoner of war and pin back my arms,
my legs. And wild with the need to help
my sons, if I dare lift my head, they
pull me down by the hair. If I move an arm,
that press of women makes me helpless, helpless.

And finally, pain beyond pain,
they do their worst. Oh my eyes, eyes that had
just looked on death—they take their brooches,
stab my eyes, make the blood pour. Then they scatter   1250
and run like fugitives.
        But I spring.
Like a beast of prey I chase those bloodthirsty bitches,

I beat at their cover like the master of the pack,
flailing, pounding.
                    And striving to do you a favor,
Agamemnon, I who killed your enemy am
made to suffer.

                    I need say little more.
Women—if they are called vile   1260
by generations past, present, or yet to come,
I can put the whole truth in a few short words:
neither sea nor earth rears another such brood.
Any man who takes his chances with them knows that
                                                        well.

CHORUSLEADER Do not be brash. Do not blame womankind
for woes you bring upon yourself. We are
a multitude, some envied for our worth,
some caught in evils that we can't escape.

HECUBA Agamemnon, a person's tongue should never
speak more loudly than his acts.   1270
Yes, if good is truly done, words must ring true;
if evil, then words must fail in strength.
No one should ever speak well of injustice.
Clever minds, of course, know how to lie,
but cleverness does not sustain them in the end.
They die ugly deaths. Not one escapes.

So much for opening remarks. Now
I shall answer this man's arguments.

                                        (*to* POLYMESTOR)

You say that you removed a twofold threat—
    Troy risen and the war renewed,   1280
and so, for Agamemnon's special benefit,
    you killed my son.
But your corrupt heart knows that Greeks have never

72

looked with friendship on barbarians.
They cannot. What is this "striving to do a favor"
that so excites your zeal? To marry a Greek?
To exert a claim of kinship? What *is* your reason?
That, should Greeks sail again, they'd devastate
your crops? Whom will your reasoning persuade?
If only you were willing to tell the truth,   1290
that gold and your own greed killed my son.

Now answer us this: Why, when chance shone bright on
                                            Troy
and walls with towers still embraced the city
and Priam lived and Hector's spear exulted,
why not then—if you wished to do this man a favor,
then, while you reared my son and sheltered him,
why not kill him then,
            or take him prisoner to the Greeks?
But you waited till the enemy snuffed out our light,
till smoke gave its signal over the city.   1300
Only then did you kill the guest at your hearth.

Keep listening.
            I charge you with further baseness.
If you were indeed the Greeks' true friend,
duty bound you to give them the gold
you admit was not yours but held in trust.
You should have brought it to them in their need
that comes from long and homesick years of war.
But no, your spirit fails.
            Not even now will your hands   1310
let go. You keep it hoarded in your house.

And had you reared my son as duty bound you,
had you saved him, how beautifully
            your name would ring.
For ugly times most clearly show our true friends,
while success attracts friends to itself.
And had you needed money while he prospered,

you would have found my son an ample treasure chest.
But now you do not have him for a friend,
your profit from the gold is gone, so are your sons,   1320
and you must live on as you are.

(*to* AGAMEMNON)

                        And I charge
that if you help him, Agamemnon,
      you, too, are criminal.
For you will benefit a host who is not reverent,
not faithful to his guest, not godly, not just.
Then we might say you also relish crimes, for you
connive at them. But you are my master.
      I mean no rebuke.

CHORUS True, how true that a righteous cause is   1330
always fertile soil for righteous words.

AGAMEMNON It burdens me to judge wrongs done by others,
but the need constrains me. To set hands on duty
and then withdraw brings a man shame.

You should know my opinion.
      You killed a boy, your guest,
not to do me a favor, not for the Greeks at all.
No, you wanted only to keep *his* gold.
And your corruption speaks only to serve itself.
Among *your* people, perhaps it's easy   1340
      to murder guests.
To us, the Greeks, this deed is ugly in its shame.
If I find you not guilty, how do I flee censure?
I can't. Because you dared act without beauty,
you must live without friendship.

POLYMESTOR What now?
      You'd have me knuckle under to a woman,
a slave. I am punished by criminals.

HECUBA   Given your crimes, is the punishment not just?

POLYMESTOR   What now?   1350
                 My children gone, my eyes made blind.

HECUBA   You grieve. And I? Do you suppose I feel no grief?

POLYMESTOR   Does it please you to mock me?

HECUBA   Why not be pleased? I have my revenge.

POLYMESTOR   *But soon, no pleasure when the sea's waves—*

HECUBA   Will take me voyaging to Greece?

POLYMESTOR   *—shall bury you after you fall from a mast.*

HECUBA   Who will force me to take that plunge?

POLYMESTOR   *You yourself shall climb the ship's mast.*

HECUBA   And how? Sprout wings on my shoulders?   1360

POLYMESTOR   *You shall become a dog, your eyes blazing fire.*

HECUBA   But how do you know my shape will change?

POLYMESTOR   Dionysos, prophet and god, so spoke.

HECUBA   But did not prophesy your own plight?

POLYMESTOR   No, or you would not have trapped me.

HECUBA   Dead or alive—just how do I reach my shore?

POLYMESTOR   *Dead. And your tomb shall be given a name—*

HECUBA   For my new shape? What are you promising?

POLYMESTOR   *—Poor Bitch's Rock, a landmark for sailors.*

HECUBA I cannot care. Justice is mine.   1370

POLYMESTOR *And your Cassandra shall be constrained to die.*

HECUBA Hateful words—I spit them back at you.

POLYMESTOR (*indicating* AGAMEMNON) *This man's wife, fierce defender*
                                                    of his house,
        shall kill her.

HECUBA May such madness never touch Clytemnestra.

POLYMESTOR *And kill him, too. He shall die by the axe.*

AGAMEMNON You—are you crazy? Begging for trouble?

POLYMESTOR Kill me. The bath of blood still waits for you.

AGAMEMNON (*to his escort*) Haul him away. Don't be gentle.

          The escort seizes POLYMESTOR *and begins to take him*
                                              away left.

POLYMESTOR It hurts you to listen?   1380

AGAMEMNON   Strap his mouth.

POLYMESTOR It's shut. I'm done with words.

AGAMEMNON   Take him.
        Throw him on some deserted island.
        He's far too brash at spouting lies.

          The escort, carrying POLYMESTOR, *exits left.*

                              (*to* HECUBA *and her women*)

        And Hecuba—Hecuba, I give you leave
        to bury your two corpses.

                         Women of Troy,
you must go to your masters' tents. The breeze
is freshening at last. We're going home.   1390

                            (looking left toward the sea)

May fair winds fill the sails. May we see
our homes again. Our troubles are done.

CHORUS Go to the harbor, my sisters.
         New trials await in our masters' tents.
         Heaven's constraint
                  is hard.

                        ALL *exit slowly left.*

NOTES ON THE TEXT
GLOSSARY

NOTES ON THE TEXT

1–65 *I come . . . the riches lost* Polydorus' ghost is not especially spectral (like Marley's) or impressive (like Hamlet's father or the ghost of King Darius in Aeschylus' *Persians*). What we *see*, I believe, is a youth of twelve or fourteen, simply dressed, with a death-pale mask; he enters and exits like anyone else. What we are to *imagine* is something different: a disembodied spirit. hovering over Hecuba in her dreams, and wanting, like all wandering ghosts, a proper burial.

24 *Troy met ruin* Troy's fall, in the tenth year of the war, was described in lost Greek poems like Arctinus' *Sack of Troy;* our vivid impressions of the Wooden Horse, Laocöon, Priam's death, the burning of Troy, and Aeneas's flight come mostly from the second book of Virgil's *Aeneid*. Euripides imagines the smoke from Troy's flames still visible from across the water.

28 *Achilles' murder-stained son* Neoptolemus, or Pyrrhus, often depicted as more violent and ruthless than his father. His murder of Priam at the altar, violating sanctuary, was one of those actions of the Greek victors that offended even gods on the Greek side. This is the man who will sacrifice Polyxena.

41–42 *And all the Greeks, becalmed . . . a fair wind* It is implied, though never clearly stated, that Achilles' ghost stopped the winds from blowing in order to compel Polyxena's sacrifice; compare Neoptolemus' later prayer (ll. 570–73) that his father allow the ships to sail. The winds do not blow, however, until the play's end. In general, Euripides plays down the supernatural element in *Hecuba* in order to place more weight on

human nature and human responsibility; but the parallel with Aulis—
where Artemis stopped the winds and the Greek fleet could not sail for
Troy until Agamemnon sacrificed his daughter, Iphigenia—is not for-
gotten.

46–47 He *claims my sister Polyxena . . . a last prize*   Appearances of Achilles'
ghost—to demand this sacrifice and/or to convey useful information to
the Greeks—were described in lost epic and lyric poems relating to the
sack of Troy and also (it seems) in an impressive account in Sophocles'
lost tragedy *Polyxena*. A separate iconographic tradition has Achilles
encountering Polyxena and her brother, Troilus, by a fountain: He
ambushes and kills Troilus, while Polyxena runs away. How early were
tales extant of Achilles' love for Polyxena, by whose hand he was
betrayed and killed? We cannot be sure, but such an erotic element may
lie behind the demanded sacrifice and the motif—more extensively
developed by Seneca in his *Troades*—of marriage with the dead.

48–58 *And it shall come to pass . . . shall come to pass*   The words here italicized
are prophetic.

55 *For the gods below*   These are Hades (or Pluto) and Persephone, king and queen of
the dead. They are represented here as unusually considerate.

94–96 *For I saw a fawn . . . from my lap*   The dream is significant and truthful in
its symbolism. Hecuba fears most strongly for Polyxena's safety, yet the
imagery of wolf rending fawn applies better to Polymestor's murder of
Polydorus, which has already taken place. Images of wild beasts recur
frequently in the play's second half.

121–23 *—He shouted, he howled . . . its last prize*   In life, Achilles cared passionately for his honor; his wrath, after Agamemnon takes his prize and war
captive, Briseis, is a chief theme of Homer's *Iliad*. In death, his
demanding nature is still felt. The Greeks won't refuse him twice.

129 *the one who is quick*   Cassandra, the daughter of Priam and Hecuba, was
courted by the god Apollo, who bestowed on her the gift of prophecy;
later, when she refused him, he added the corollary that no one would
believe her. Now Agamemnon has taken her as his mistress. He will
bring her home to Argos, where, not surprisingly, his wife Clytemnestra
will murder them both.

131 *Theseus' two sons*   Their names were Acamas and Demophon. Athenian legend depicts them as noble and generous; their ruthlessness here savors of modern-day Athens, as the Achaean assembly is transformed into something like the Athenian.

143 *son of Laertes*   This is Odysseus. Like a modern-day Athenian politician and demagogue, he controls the assembly's debate for his own purposes. The words used of him are colloquial and insulting.

258–60 *Remember when you came . . . in your beard*   Odysseus disguised himself as a beggar to spy upon Troy. As Helen tells the story (Homer's *Odyssey*, 4, 240–64), she alone recognized Odysseus, but she helped him because her mind and heart had returned to their former Greek allegiance. If, as Euripides has it, Helen told Hecuba, then Hecuba can only have spared Odysseus out of compassion—very misplaced compassion, from the Trojan point of view!

274–75 *You people who grew up . . . crowd-coaxing tongues*   Again, this recalls the Athenian politicians of Euripides' day as a disgruntled aristocrat might view them.

286 *Helen*   Her beauty launched the "thousand ships." Paris, backed by Aphrodite, carried her off from her husband, Menelaus, whose brother, Agamemnon, led the great expedition to punish the Trojans and bring her home. Homer pictures her as beautiful but repentant; in Greek tragedy she more often appears beautiful, irresponsible, and guilty, an instrument employed by the gods to demonstrate the workings of justice, wreak havoc with human lives, or reduce the surplus population. (Euripides' play *Helen* where she is presented as innocent, is a remarkable exception.) In *Hecuba* the guilty Helen is contrasted with the innocent Polyxena.

296 *I cling, I touch*   Through these formal gestures, the suppliant begs for help and protection in the gods' names. To refuse a suppliant was not just inconsiderate but dangerous.

303–6 *The strong should not abuse . . . lost*   Hecuba's plea ironically recalls the warnings Odysseus addresses to Penelope's suitors in the *Odyssey* (17, 414–44; 18, 124–50), warnings that reflect his own tragic experience and the mature wisdom he has gained since the fall of Troy.

366 *for he has children*   Actually, Odysseus had only one child, his son Telemachus, whom he loved dearly.

487–90 *The isle where . . . twin children*   Delos, formerly a floating island, welcomed Leto when, pregnant by Zeus, she was pursued by Hera's hostility. There, holding onto a palm tree, she gave birth to the bright gods Apollo and Artemis. The laurel became Apollo's sacred tree. In the *Odyssey* (6, 160–68) the needy Odysseus compares the princess Nausicaä to a beautiful palm tree he once saw at Delos—a picture of just and beautiful human growth that Euripides remembers and uses.

495 *Athena's saffron robe*   A highlight of the annual *Panathenaea* (held at the end of July, according to our calendar) was the presentation of a new robe, or *peplos,* to cover the great cult statue of Athena in her temple (Erechtheum) on the Acropolis. We still catch something of the beauty and excitement of this festival from the great procession depicted on the Parthenon frieze (housed in the British Museum in London). The *peplos* was woven by Athenian maidens during the preceding year. Its size, bright colors, and tapestrylike decorations were impressive. Just how Trojan slaves might find comfort in such a spectacle, or at Delos, is not clear.

500–502 *Or shall I weave Titans . . . death*   Zeus' victory over the Titans, those violent nature spirits, is described in Hesiod's *Theogony*. This struggle came to symbolize the triumph of civilization over savagery in human life, hence serving as a mythic foil to the present tragedy.

518 *falsely sure*   The line here bracketed is probably an actor's interpolation or, less likely, a critic's explanation that has been absorbed into the text. If we retain it, then Talthybius is displaying even greater skepticism by asking not only whether the gods watch over human lives but whether they exist in the first place. From a practical Greek standpoint, the difference is not significant.

552–613 *They were all there . . . the brightest in soul*   Human sacrifice, long since abolished in Greece, is frequently practiced in myth and drama to avert a god's anger and/or to win a victory. The voluntary sacrifice of a virgin is especially potent; by assenting, Polyxena here transforms her necessary death into a beautiful act that even the Greeks admire.

564–65 *"Silence, Greeks . . . Silence"*   Euripides' audience, too, will be hushed in silence, paying careful attention to the narrative.

573–75 *safe return home* . . . *"Safe return home"* This part of the prayer would not be fulfilled. Ajax, the son of Oileus, was shipwrecked; Agamemnon was murdered upon reaching home; others (most notably Odysseus) suffered delays and hardships at sea and found new troubles awaiting them at home. Neoptolemus, the speaker, returns home and lives happily for a while until he is killed at Delphi by Apollo's attendant priests and at Orestes' instigation. In general, dark irony hangs over the fates of the Greek victors in Euripides' Trojan plays.

636 *Do parents count* In Euripides' time Hecuba's questions were posed by "sophists," those traveling professors who taught courses in political science, economics, or rhetoric to the ambitious sons of rich Athenians, and are restated brilliantly in Plato's early dialogues: (a) Can *aretê* (virtue, excellence) be taught? (b) How much of *aretê* is inborn (*physis, phya*) and inherited, and how much is the result of upbringing (*trophê*), instruction (*didachê*), and one's environment? (c) How can a good and noble upbringing serve as an instructive model about what is ignoble and bad? The old aristocratic belief in inherited nobility, supplemented by proper training, is best conveyed in Pindar's victory odes; in general, it is challenged by the new professors, the would-be educators of Athenian youth. Hecuba speaks for the old ways, but her thinking, like that of Euripides, is infused with the new.

649–50 *For the last time* . . . *virgin's ghost* Often in Greek tragedy, imagery of the "marriage with death" contrasts a virgin's untimely funeral with the bright hopes of marriage. On her wedding day, a bride's mother bathes her in water drawn from a sacred spring.

667–93 *My fate* . . . *her sacrifice* Chronological time passes swiftly during this ode, which reviews the Paris–Helen story but reverses the order of events. In the fateful beauty contest on Mt. Ida, Paris judged not Hera or Athena most beautiful but Aphrodite, who offered him the most attractive woman in Greece as his wife. He then sailed to Greece and carried off Helen with Aphrodite's help, thus causing war and grief.

722–24 *I'll raise you a song* . . . *new strains of grief* The Greek text here is disputed (we follow Daitz [Stephen G. Daitz (Leipzig, 1973)]), but the ambiguity seems clear: the *"nomon baccheion ex alastoros"* that Hecuba now commences is either a Bacchic "strain" or a new Bacchic "law" created by an avenging spirit, or *alastor*.

776–91 HECUBA (aside)   She is playing for effect. All her "spontaneous" doubts are orchestrated for Agamemnon's benefit.

841–43 *the law of custom . . . right from wrong*   The Greek text plays on the ambiguity of *nomos*, which can mean "law," "custom," or both. Does Hecuba mean that the law is an underlying principle of existence, overriding even the gods' will, and governing human life in its religious and social aspects? Or does she mean that it is merely a result of convention and custom that we believe in the gods and make moral distinctions to regulate our lives? The ambiguity suggests that Hecuba's public and private views of the world no longer coincide.

858 *Why do we spend*   Another allusion to the sophists. The "art of persuasion" brought quick successes in the assembly and the law courts. Its best-known teacher was the Sicilian orator Gorgias of Leontini, who visited Athens in 427, as well as at other times, and left a great impression.

893–97 *What does it mean? . . . once meant well*   In this difficult passage, the chorus appears to be saying both that everything "comes together" or "falls into confusion" for mortals, and that customs and laws (*nomoi*), provide a framework for necessary situations; among these, presumably, is the transformation of enemies into friends and vice-versa. Apparently language and customs are like a veil drawn over what can't be grasped, namely, the shifting realities or "necessities" of human life.

908–10 *The army thinks . . . by the army*   The army is represented, in un-Homeric fashion, as an unruly mob. In the latter part of the fifth century, even reputable Athenian generals could be slandered by unscrupulous politicians (which hardly helped the war effort).

916–19 *For some are slaves . . . the crowd's beliefs*   Again Euripides makes Hecuba echo a significant and dangerous modern debate: the case of natural freedom versus social and conventional restraints. The latter are represented here as imposed by the ruling democratic "majority" in the form of written laws (which are subject to change) enacted by that majority. Hecuba sneers at the "crowd" as an aristocrat might (in private), much as she denounced demagogues earlier. The oligarchic revolutions of 411 and 404 B.C. would prove how insidious this appeal to "freedom" can be; the sentiments would also be voiced by the Nietzschean figures in Plato's dialogues.

938–39 *What! Did not women . . . every last male* Hecuba's defense of women underscores their propensity for violence. The fifty Danaids, daughters of Danaus, fled to Argos, where they were pursued by their Egyptian cousins and forced to wed them. Forty-nine, at Danaus' instigation, killed their husbands on their wedding night and were condemned to fill leaky jars with water in Hades as punishment for their deed. The women of Lemnos also killed their husbands and lived for a time without male companionship.

959–1005 *You . . . her fathers' home* The women sing of the night when Troy was captured. The Trojans had celebrated the (pretended) departure of the Greeks with song, dance, and great festivity, but all this was a delusion. The Greeks sailed back from the island of Tenedos, where they had been hiding. Their leaders emerged from the Wooden Horse and quickly and brutally captured the city.

During this ode, as usual, chronological time is flexible: Hecuba's messenger travels inland to find Polymestor and brings him back to the Greek camp.

977 *I was arranging my hair* Professor Arrowsmith reminds us that "slave women were normally *shorn;* these lines about how it was *before* their slavery, before their hair was shorn, are a fine instance of Euripides' refusal to use merely decorative detail, merely lovely touches of ordinary domestic life."

997 *To the sister* Helen's two brothers were the demigods Castor and Polydeuces (Pollux), the twin Dioscuri, or "sons of Zeus." In Greek lore they became figures of salvation, especially for sailors caught in storms at sea. Helen lived with Paris (who had been raised as a shepherd on Mt. Ida) but was not, strictly speaking, his wife.

1005 *May she never return* She did, of course, return. In the fourth book of the *Odyssey,* when she and Menelaus entertain Telemachus in Sparta, Helen looks back on her Trojan period as a kind of temporary aberration. Menelaus is not so sure.

1006–76 *My dearest friend . . . housed my child* The following scene is heavily ironic, with concealed knowledge on both sides; hence the presence of many ambiguous remarks.

1011–13 *And it's the gods . . . will worship them* The Greek words are ambiguous: the gods put confusion in things so that we may worship them "through ignorance." Does Polymestor mean through ignorance of what is happening in men's lives or, more sophistically, by falsely imagining that the gods exist, when enlightened people like Polymestor know they don't?

1047 *visit you in secret*   The irony backfires; Polydorus' ghost had made his own arrangements.

1095 *I'll batter these walls.*   Euripides' lines do not make the staging clear. Line 1096 (1041 in the Greek), which Daitz gives to Polymestor, literally means "See! A missile is launched from a heavy hand." The words follow (or are followed by) a loud noise, as of a heavy object striking a wall—the wooden wall, in fact, of the stage building, here represented as a tent or hut. Polymestor is wildly attempting either to hit his enemies or to escape.

1113–14 POLYMESTOR stumbles   The blinding of Polymestor will recall the ninth book of the *Odyssey,* where the man-eating cyclops Polyphemus is tricked and blinded by Odysseus, emerging as an almost pitiable figure, though still a dangerous one. Euripides' one surviving satyr play, the *Cyclops,* presents a farcical version of these events. The blinded giant is teased by the chorus of childish satyrs, as in a game of blind-man's buff. Quite possibly the *Cyclops* formed part of the same tetralogy as *Hecuba,* providing comic relief but also reflecting serious themes from *Hecuba* in the distorting mirror of farce.

1139 *soon torn apart*   The image is literally false but symbolically true, since it compares Hecuba and her women to Dionysus' maenads, his ecstatic female followers, who in the course of their rituals rend wild animals and eat them raw (*sparagmos, ômophagia*), and who could, in their frenzy, do the same to humans (compare Euripides' *Bacchae*).

1170 *Dog Star at heel*   Sirius, the Dog Star, suggests the burning heat of summer. Polymestor's lyrical wish to lose himself in the sky or sea is conveyed in images that anticipate Hecuba's eventual fate as a fiery-eyed hellhound plunging from the ship's mast into the sea (see ll. 1355–61).

1206–1329 *Argue your case . . . no rebuke*   This heralds a formal debate (*agôn*) such as the Athenians always enjoyed both in real life as well as on the tragic or comic stage. The latter debater usually wins. Polymestor speaks as the plaintiff, the injured party, but also defends his killing of

Polydorus. Hecuba rebuts his arguments—and scarcely bothers to defend her own behavior.

1265–68 *Do not be brash . . . we can't escape*   The chorusleader, speaking for the women of the chorus (and probably for Euripides), warns Polymestor not to indulge in rash generalizations about women. Lines 1185–86 in the Greek ("We are . . . can't escape") were deleted by Dindorf (G. Dindorf [Greek text], Oxford, 1832); they are bracketed in Murray's Oxford text (1902) as an actor's interpolation; their meaning is uncertain. We follow Daitz's text and punctuation in all other respects but read *tôn kakôn:* "Some women are enviable" (i.e., for their virtue); "others of us are born by nature into the number of the bad." Euripides touches briefly here on the unfair lot of women, who are to be envied or else considered evil. In his lifetime he was satirized as a misogynist, always depicting evil women and shaming good ones. Our translation highlights the relevance of these remarks to Polyxena and Hecuba.

1355–76 *But soon . . . die by the axe*   The passages here italicized are in the form of a prophecy. Polymestor speaks with new insight and authority, rather like Sophocles' blinded Oedipus; but his inspiration is Dionysian, not Apollonian, and all he foresees is bestial transformation and murder.

1369 Poor Bitch's Rock   Greek *Cynossema,* from *kyôn,* "dog" (the term "bitch" is often insulting in Greek, as in English), and *sêma,* a "sign" or "tomb." Cynossema became the name of a Thracian promontory.

1371–76 *And your Cassandra . . . die by the axe*   The audience knew the sequel well from epic, lyric, and tragic works (notably, for modern readers, in Aeschylus's *Agamemnon*). Clytemnestra killed Cassandra and Agamemnon partly for revenge (besides bringing his mistress home, Agamemnon had sacrificed their daughter Iphigenia) and partly to please her lover, Aegisthus. One version had Agamemnon butchered at the feast; another had him ensnared in the bathtub and killed—hardly a suitable end, either way, for the great victor at Troy.

1395–96 *Heaven's constraint is hard*   The last word, *anankē,* usually translated as "Necessity," suggests a harsh and impersonal controlling power determining the course of human events. We have translated it throughout the play as "constraint," which, according to the OED, denotes "coercion or compulsion," or (by transference) "confinement, bound or fettered condition, restriction of liberty or of free action"; other meanings, now obsolete, are "oppression, affliction, distress." All this suggests the thematic range of *anankē* in Euripides' play, as well as its affinities, as Professor Arrowsmith has pointed out, with such words as "angst," "anguish," and "angina."

GLOSSARY

ACHILLES: the greatest Greek warrior who fought at Troy; he killed Hector and was subsequently killed by Paris.

AGAMEMNON: king of Mycenae, or Argos; brother of Menelaus; leader of the Greek expedition against Troy. He sacrificed his daughter Iphigenia to avert Artemis' anger so that the winds might blow again and permit the ships to sail to Troy. His wife, Clytemnestra, killed him upon his return home, aided by her lover Aegisthus. Agamemnon's death was avenged by his son, Orestes, and his daughter, Electra.

ARTEMIS: goddess of wildlife; helper of women in childbirth.

ATHENA: goddess of wisdom and crafts; goddess of war; patron goddess of Athens.

ATREUS: king of Mycenae, father of Agamemnon and Menelaus.

CASSANDRA: daughter of Priam and Hecuba, whose prophecies, inspired by Apollo, were never believed. Raped by Ajax and abducted by Agamemnon as his mistress, she was later killed, together with him, by Clytemnestra.

DELOS: small island in the Aegean Cyclades; birthplace of the twins Apollo and Artemis.

HADES: brother of Zeus and ruler of the Underworld; his name is synonymous with death.

HECTOR: son of Priam and Hecuba; husband of Andromache and father of Astyanax: champion of Troy, he was eventually slain by Achilles.

HECUBA: queen of Troy and wife of Priam; mother of, among others, Hector, Cassandra, Polyxena, and Polydorus.

HELEN: daughter of Zeus and Leda and wife of Menelaus, king of Sparta; her elopement with Paris was the cause of the Trojan War.

HELENUS: son of Priam and Hecuba; like Cassandra, he possessed the gift of prophecy.

IDA: mountain range near Troy.

LAERTES: father of Odysseus.

LETO: mother, by Zeus, of Apollo and Artemis.

ODYSSEUS: son of Laertes, king of Ithaca, where he returned successfully in the twentieth year after leaving for Troy.

PALLAS: another name for the goddess Athena.

PERSEPHONE: "corn maiden"; daughter of Zeus and Demeter, wife of Hades, and queen of the Underworld.

PHTHIA: town in Thessaly (in northern Greece); home of Achilles.

POLYDORUS: youngest son of Priam and Hecuba; he was murdered by the Thracian king Polymestor, to whom his parents had entrusted him, along with much gold.

POLYMESTOR: treacherous Thracian king; formerly the guest-friend of Priam and Hecuba.

POLYXENA: daughter of Priam and Hecuba; demanded in sacrifice by Achilles' ghost.

PRIAM: king of Troy; he was killed at the altar by Achilles' son, Neoptolemus (or Pyrrhus); a paradigm of human happiness turned to misery.

TALTHYBIUS: Greek herald, model of decency.

THESEUS: legendary king of Athens; father of Acamas and Demophon; famous for killing evildoers.

THRACE: vast northern region, controlled by competing warlike tribes, whose southern coast on the Aegean sea and the Propontis was colonized by Greeks.

TITANS: elemental powers; an older race of gods conquered by Zeus and imprisoned; their king was Kronos (Roman god Saturn).

TROY: city in northwestern Asia Minor.

ZEUS: king of gods and men (Roman god Jupiter); often represented as the protector of guest-friends and suppliants.